Divine Focus

By Yvonne Prentice

Copyright

Dedication

This Book is dedicated to the One who is present to every generation in every moment of time.

May we all live in the realization of the presence of God the Father, God the Son (Jesus Christ) and God the Spirit.

My prayer is that future generations will live with anticipation of experiencing God's presence with them each moment.

Acknowledgments

My greatest joy and fulfillment are that I am chosen as a child of God. I want to give honour to My Heavenly Father, to the Lord Jesus Christ and to the Spirit of God, for allowing me the privilege of doing this work with Him. We have shared beautiful times and difficult times as I learned and grew into writing what you are about to read.

I am so thankful to my dear family and friends who have loved, encouraged, and supported me through the years it has taken to complete this project. I have been helped by many of you through the years, your patience is such a blessing to me.

Thank you so much Laura King for giving your time to the editorial work. You are such a beautiful example of humility and selflessness.

Thanks to my daughter Abigail Cook who gave artistic advice for the sketches. They came alive because of your input.

I give special thanks to my publisher and friend, Serenity McLean. The cover of this book and the other five books you have designed for me are beautifully done, inspired by God. Your many hours of patient help have been a treasure to me. You are an answer to prayer.

I thank God for all the saints who have laid a foundation of spiritual practice for us to follow. The road to divine focus is rich, because God's people desired to know Him, found ways to practice His presence and passed them on to us.

Last, but not at all least, I want to thank God for my dear husband Bob. Your love and tenderness toward Jesus inspire me. You are truly my soul mate. My heart is full of love and thanks for you.

Contents

Introduction

For centuries, followers of Jesus Christ have struggled in their quest to know God. In this quest they learned to overcome the pressures, persecutions and enticements of life on earth. These forerunners of faith discovered truths, principals, and practices that oiled their journey toward intimacy with God. This trilogy presents wisdom they discovered and utilized to commune with God. Some of these ideas and practices have been almost forgotten or passed over. The evidence of this loss is the current epidemic of apathy and disconnection many suffer. There is, however, a desire rising among believers to know and experience God deeply. Holy Spirit is brooding over the void of mediocrity in the Church to revive and impassion our generation. Divine Focus will bring motivation, foundation, clarity and spiritual tools to the aid of those who long to live in divine union with God.

To begin our exploration into the subject of focusing all of our human faculties (spirit, soul and body) toward God, it seems appropriate, even Holy Spirit directed, to consider this topic through the lens of Jesus' personal description of himself. Jesus describes himself with three words. He says that He is the Way, He is the Truth and He is the Life. (John 14:6) I have chosen to arrange the topics in reverse order. Each of these titles is equally significant as we consider the subject of connecting with our magnificent maker. Yet, to begin at the beginning it seems fitting to talk about the perfect life of focus modeled by Jesus himself.

You will note at the end of each chapter 'listening prayer/ meditation' exercises. To make this a personal journey into deepening friendship with God, I recommend taking the time as you read to experience God. Times of quiet contemplation, practicing the disciplines and asking God the questions provided will enhance the journey. Keeping a personal journal of your discoveries and the things God reveals to you will help you to integrate His thoughts into your daily life.

One way to work through the listening prayer exercises is to employ the suggestions for practices and disciplines in the final section. For example, one could take the first question to the Lord through soaking prayer, contemplating over an extended period. After soaking write out what was experienced during the session. The experience that occurred (whether it be a series of feelings, thoughts, emotions, or pictures) will be, in some form, an answer to the question for contemplation. In this way one could work through the suggested listening prayer questions. Experimenting with the disciplines and practices helps us to find which best suit our personality, lifestyle and needs.

Practicing the presence of God in our current time in history has become more challenging than it was for our forefathers and mothers. Our lives are fragmented and our attention extremely divided due to the modern conveniences of technology that none of us could do without. But God has not changed. He still loves us. He still is waiting with longsuffering patience to embrace His beloved sons and daughters. He is not satisfied with a snippet of our attention as we dash into our day. God longs for deep connection, even oneness with our hearts, as He always has. Will we stop and take in the moment to find His gaze? Can we find the time and attention required to know Him well? My prayer is that you will engage with Him as you read, ponder and pray through the book. There is a guarantee to those who will ask, seek and knock in desire for Him.

Ask and it will be given to you; seek and you will find; knock and the door will be opened to you. For everyone who asks receives; the one who seeks finds; and to the one who knocks, the door will be opened. Matt. 7:7–8

Book 1: The Life

Fern Fullness

A time-lapse video of the fiddlehead fern is such a wonder to watch. Pushing up from the womb of earth, it is born tightly furled. Its little coils move, stretch and twist in almost dance like gyrations. The life in each tiny fern is so very vibrant. Though it is not spectacular in blossom, the fern speaks to me of vibrancy and life released, as it stretches into its fully unfurled magnificence. It is so much like us I think. Born so small and tightly furled from the womb we yearn to be completely open and full in every way, and so we shall be, as we receive the rain of love and communion we are made for. As we move in the rhythms of God's life for us we surely will embrace true life and spiritual satisfaction. He will stretch us, if we will give our hearts in undivided focus and rise up to our divine purpose and destiny.

The first of the three books in this collection is titled "The Life". We begin with the last of the three descriptions Jesus gave of Himself (the Way, the Truth, and the Life). He is *The Life* laid down for our redemption. The sacrifice of His earthly life effectively and permanently connected all who choose to give their lives to God. Jesus, the life, also *lived* the example of connection with God the Father and God the Spirit. He demonstrated a lifestyle of yielded submission to the plans of His Father. He lived for the fulfillment of His earthly purpose and in so doing gave us eternal life. Not only that, Jesus is the template for living in union with God.

As we examine Jesus' example and a few of His teachings about a rightly focused life, we note the intimate relational connections He models. As Christians (Christ followers) it is our privilege to live as Jesus did. Jesus advocated that we follow Him – even that we take up our cross in sacrificially living as He did. We can, here and now, have intimate communion with our Heavenly Father, just as He did. We get to enjoy the pleasure of being one with this wonderful God! We are privileged to know and live His individual purpose for our creation. We can, to an even greater degree, walk with God in communion each day as Adam and Eve did in the garden.

This spiritual treasure (of being one with God) is indeed the inheritance Jesus left for us. The gift of His Divine nature is available, to be fully enjoyed by the people of God. It is indeed the abundant life that Jesus has given to all mankind, but only those who choose to follow and yield to Him will avail themselves of it. Choosing abundant life over mediocrity seems a given. Who would choose mediocrity? Surprisingly many, because it is the choice by default. We step into abundant, full and vibrant destiny only when we step into the lifestyle and nature of Jesus Christ.

That is why the first book of this trilogy is to examine the example and teachings of our amazing mentor Jesus. He blazed the trail, both by example and by devotion to continual focus on the Father. He did those things as a mortal man. Though He is God, He laid aside His deity to live as we must live, a human soul fused to Holy Spirit. This sacrifice, though it was extreme, has extreme benefits to us, in that we can see how God would operate if He was made into human form. I can't fathom the love it took to leave Heaven's freedom and beauty to live among a people who would dishonour and even murder you.

Such extreme love and commitment is deeply touching and indeed supernatural. Even more astounding is the fact that God knew full well what it would take to rescue us and move us from the darkness and bondage of our sin into to the light and freedom of His kingdom.

So, lets ponder together our fearless leader and allow Holy Spirit to mentor us along the way. The following is just a small taste to whet your appetite for what I pray will be your life's pleasure – to know this amazing One and live in union with His Spirit.

1 – Perfect Life

No one has a perfect life! Ever since the fall of mankind, life on planet earth has been hard. In fact, it was the original sin with which we all are lumbered that set the world on a very different axis. That is the world we live in today and that is the world Jesus came to save. If it were perfect, God would not have needed to redeem it. If we were perfect we would still be living in unbroken friendship with Him today. Jesus is perfection personified, but he had to slug it out in the difficulties of the planet just as we do. In fact, the world when he came was full of disease, bloodshed and suffering. I'm thinking He felt it all just as we do. There are a lot of things missing from the accounts of Jesus life in the gospels. We are not told if he ever had a virus or if he bloodied his knees as a child. Did his new sandals give him blisters? Did he shiver and swelter like the rest of us do? I think He did. I think Jesus suffered all the inconveniences, and more than we do. He had frustration, anger and grief even more than we can imagine. But He overcame and lived it out perfectly. That is the point, is it not? Not that he never felt the sting or joys in human life but he handled it all perfectly. He loved in the face of extreme hatred. He rejoiced and laughed in pure joy. He cried and grieved with sincerity, but He had hope. He is hope.

This perfect life overcame every barrier to love, joy, peace, gentleness, goodness, humility, faith and focus. He is willing to keep doing it, through you and me. Lets follow this thread to see where Holy Spirit will take us. Picture yourself with Him as we enter into this glimpse of perfect life.

People came to listen to Jesus by the thousands because He not only spoke truth that resonated with them, but He proved the authority of those words by the power of God. He performed miracles, healings, and signs that made people wonder. Words that carry weight have a way of shaking us; causing shifts in our thinking. Weighty words with actions demonstrating their validity are even more potent. They change our focus. Jesus words changed those who would receive them, for good. His words are still changing people today.

The example Jesus set is our template as His followers. Something basic that we see in Jesus life is that He lived focused on His Father (God). The Father's Heart for the world, the Fathers timing and agenda, were never compromised. Human need surrounded Jesus day and night. Human and supernatural pressure, along with threats and intimidation, always loomed close by. Accolades and flattery, designed to tempt Him, came at times of extreme vulnerability. All these things, as well as the ultimate and very real threat – that of death itself, did not deter Jesus or steal His focus from the Father.

We may think Jesus ability to focus was supernatural. That is correct, but it was not Jesus deity that enabled Him at that time. Jesus tapped into the Holy Spirit's empowerment to give Him the undivided focus that sustained Him. That same power is available to us, in the same measure, as Jesus had. Our King Jesus came to show us how to live so that we could do even greater works than He did. John 14:12 Jesus connected with His Father in heaven just as we have to today. Holy Spirit enabled Him; remember His water/Spirit baptism by John the Baptist. Jesus only did what He saw His Father do and heard His Father say.

Jesus gave them this answer: "Very truly I tell you, the Son can do nothing by himself; he can do only what he sees his Father doing, because whatever the Father does the Son also does." John 5:19

Ponder that for a moment. Where was the Father when Jesus was looking and listening? The Father was in this heavenly throne room and Jesus was at that time on earth. In order for Jesus to connect by seeing and hearing His Father Jesus had to look in the spirit and listen by the Spirit just as we have to today. We can follow His example if we choose to, by the power of His enabling Holy Spirit. We can today use the same level of focus Jesus employed to connect with God.

Focus is undivided attention with all of our heart, soul, mind, and strength. It is a gift we, who belong to His kingdom, are given. Jesus told us how:

"Seek and you shall find, ask and you shall receive, knock and the door will be opened to you." Matthew 7:7

He modeled a life of time spent in the presence of His Father. It is that living relationship of close connection that produces the nature of Jesus Christ in us. Jesus said we would do even greater works than He, therefore we need to do as He did. We need to live a life of attention toward our Father, to spend daily time alone to hear and see what He has for us. Draw near to God by His Spirit, the one who gives us all we need for life and Godliness. As we live attuned to the Holy Spirit within us, the Spirit flows throughout our spirit, soul and body to produce Christ in us.

2 – Glory Contained

We are vessels containing the Glory of God (Holy Spirit). Holy Spirit unifies our lives with God. The Spirit is the essence of Christ. It is God's design that we carry the Spirit of Christ on earth so as to be His embodiment.

> *The mystery that has been kept hidden for ages and generations, but is now disclosed to the saints. To them God has chosen to make known among the Gentiles the glorious riches of this mystery, which is Christ in you, the hope of glory. Colossians 1:26–27*

This glory is the divine essence through which we can commune with God and also display the nature and character of Christ to the world. We are the body of Christ on earth right now. Jesus Christ is, at this moment, seated at the right hand of God the Father and also seated on earth in us. It is indeed an amazing mystery, which He invites us to explore, grow in, and live.

Another such mystery awaiting us is written by the Apostle Paul about his and our identity in Jesus Christ;

> *I have been crucified with Christ and I no longer live, but Christ lives in me. The life I now live in the body, I live by faith in the Son of God, who loved me and gave himself for me. Galatians 2:20*

The nature of one who has received the Holy Spirit

through faith in Jesus Christ has changed. This person no longer lives as a mere human. The flesh (old carnal nature) has died with Christ. The life lived as a believer is lived knowing the fact that Jesus is their true life. The one who lives by faith is fused to Him in their spirit. Christ is living through believers as His Spirit moves and motivates from within.

> *But we have this treasure in jars of clay to show that this all-surpassing power is from God and not from us. 2 Corinthians 4:7*

We can join Paul in the wonder of knowing we have the treasure of the all-surpassing power from God in our human bodies. The value of treasure is relative to how one sees it. Family treasures are sometimes valued by one generation but dismissed by another. The saying; "one man's trash is another man's treasure", is true with eternal things as well. Though God alone knows the true worth of the deposit He has made in us, we can be assured it is priceless beyond earthly measure. It is this life-giving treasure (Holy Spirit) who is personal, powerful and productive, who is able to transform us into the likeness and image of Jesus.

Treasure

> *"But store up for yourselves treasures in heaven, where moth and rust do not destroy, and where thieves do not break in and steal. For where your treasure is there your heart will be also. Matthew 6:19–21*

Treasures are our most valued possessions. For most of us time, money, energy and attention are what we consider the most precious commodities we have. So, how are you spending those things? Ask yourself that question. Our true passion is revealed by where we invest those things. We can miss our calling and be diverted from our life's purpose if we invest our treasures in places that do not bring the right kind of return. God desires to see fruit that will last.

God has treasure too. We can tell where His heart is by where He has invested it. Ponder that thought. God invested the most precious of all he had, Jesus Christ and gave all of His essence into the salvation of mankind. That is the proof of His devotion. We are now brothers and sisters of Christ, grafted into the family of God. His divine plan was at extreme cost to the Father. Such devotion, to sacrifice the greatest possession to the most profound degree, is His eternal investment.

Listening Prayer/Meditation Exercise
In light of those thoughts ask yourself:

To what am I giving my substance?

What am I investing my time, energy, money and attention in?

3 – One Day

The day begins with Jesus teaching about the condition of Israel and faith in His teaching. Then His family comes to see Him.

Israel Asks For a Miracle

The teaching on the sign of Jonah (Matthew12:38) reveals the condition of Israel: being an evil and faithless generation because they are asking for a sign. The issue was not that they had no evidence. Jesus had been healing, performing signs and teaching revelatory concepts, but still the people wanted a miracle on their demand. Jesus never performed for people or at the command of any authority. He only did what His father asked and showed Him to do. He ultimately paid with His life for the simple act of focusing on the will of the father.

Jesus' response to the demand for a miracle was to give historical examples from the Scriptures which all would understand. First Jonah spent three days and nights buried in the great fish: Jesus told them they would see Him do the same, referring to His future death and resurrection. The other example was of the Queen of Sheba, who travelled from a distant land to hear the wisdom of an earthly King, Solomon, and Jesus' own words,

"Now someone greater than Solomon is here

and you refuse to listen to Him".

Jesus then uses the metaphor of the demonized person to represent Israel: that person was given an opportunity to begin a fresh life, once they were cleansed, but because they did not fill up with the right Spirit they ended up much worse than before. The meaning was clear; the opportunity for a fresh start was before them in the form of the new covenant God was going to make through the blood of Jesus Christ Himself. Israel could receive the good gift of deliverance from the old religious system and receive the Spirit that was soon to fill those who believed, or they would be much worse off than before.

Jesus focuses on the Father's agenda: Jesus then is told that His mother and brothers have come to see Him, but He chooses to minister to the crowd instead of going to them, saying "Who are my mother and brothers? These are my mother and brothers. Anyone who does the will of my Father in heaven is my brother and sister and mother!" It seems as though Jesus is rejecting His earthly family; however, we see at the end of the chapter that He understood their motive for coming. At that moment His place was to teach the ones who were open. Jesus again demonstrates focus at a level that can only be lived through union with the will of the Father. He knew by the Spirit that when the teaching was done He would indeed return to Nazareth and be rejected by not only His family but also by the whole town.

> But Jesus said to them. "Only in his
> hometown and in his own house is a prophet
> without honour." Matthew 13:57

He did only a few miracles there because of their unbelief. It was their unbelief not His inability. He chose to do only a few. Could it be He chose not to cast His pearls in that place knowing it would be rationalized away because of the offence they had taken to His fame. The Scripture says they were deeply offended and refused to believe in Him.

This example shows Jesus living in communion with His Father in heaven following only the Father's initiatives.

Jesus' focus on His Father's will was challenged through both encounters that day. The unbelief of those who demanded another miracle, later the unbelief of His close human family and neighbours did not deter Him from focusing on His Father. The demands and rejection of that day did not change His focus on the Father for direction, timing and wisdom. As the day goes on Jesus teaches through symbolic stories. The stories progress and deepen. Each one is significant in modeling connection with God in that time and in ours.

4 – Seven Stories from Matthew 13

These seven teachings/lessons were significant in content, in order and in regard to the audience who heard them. The number seven symbolizes perfection, coming from the perfect sinless Son of God. You will note four stories are to the people at large (4 being the number of the earth) and three stories are given to the disciples (3 being the number of divine completion). This teaching was to draw those of the population of the earth. Whoever wanted to could come and hear Jesus speak; however, the disciples were being taught the deeper revelation of kingdom values.

Every aspect of the teachings of Jesus contains amazing revelation that God is still unwrapping for us today. This small offering is just scratching the surface of what each story contains. I trust the Spirit of God to expand these wonderful truths as you meditate on the lessons Jesus taught. Perhaps you will choose to spend time with God listening or soaking about one of these spiritual story lessons Jesus taught. Here are some thoughts and observations He has shown me.

The Farmer and the Seed (Matthew 13:3–23)

There were four types of soil the farmer's seed came in contact with. Notice he sowed into all types, which I believe was on purpose. The Farmer in this story did not indiscriminately throw seed. This farmer represents God and the seed the word of God. Due to His great love and mercy, He is not willing that any should perish. We can be sure it was on purpose the seed fell where it did. Our Father offers the good seed of truth to all mankind (not a selected few).

Some seed falls on the hard path. A path symbolizes a way of life. The hard path is a lifestyle of hardened evil. Notice on the hard path that truth never gets to germinate. If sin, unbelief, and negativity are allowed, they will quickly snatch away the truth of God.

Some seed falls on the shallow rocky soil that is symbolic for hindrances and the hard issues of life. This person has a blockage keeping them from going deeper in God. At first the Christian life seems exciting, but as time goes on, the initial excitement gives way to the reality of every-day difficulties. The heat of the sun symbolizes the dry times that are meant to drive our spiritual roots deep into God. Issues of the soul can halt the progress of deepening our communion with God, if they are not dealt with. For example, unforgiveness, bitterness, judgments of others, fear, etc., can block our relationships with people and also God.

Persecution also has a way of sorting those who really love God from those who are shallow. Those who are shallow are not able to draw from His goodness or overcome obstacles. The hindrance (whether past practices, present habits, woundedness or persecution) blocks their ability to root themselves in God and they wither, often giving up.

Other seed fell among Thorns that shoot up and choke out the tender blades. Here we see people who are dominated by their situation. Whether it be the cares of this life (which surround us all), the hunger for wealth, or the choice to be among negative, thorny and abrasive people who dominate them, their tender faith is quickly overridden with their own needs. The opinions of others become more important than the word of God to them. This group of new believers can be dominated by people and circumstances that appear to them stronger than the life of faith. All of these things steal away the genuine friendship with God.

Of course, the good fertile soil represents those who have a hunger for God and a desire to go deeper with Him. It is interesting to note that any of the issues the other types of seeds had can be remedied with the power of God. We can, by choice, remove ourselves from the hard path (living in agreement with the enemy). Jesus has all power to deliver whoever asks. The shallow individual can repent of the blockages in their lives and ask to go deeper. God will always answer that prayer when it is accompanied with the desire for change. The thorns are actually all around everyone – the cares of this life, money issues and negative dominating people. The answer is to focus on Jesus and follow His empowered life through the Spirit. Then we can be good, fertile people of God.

Looking at the numbers Jesus chose to use for the amounts of increase, we see that the seed produced in the good soil is thirty. This is the number for training, sorrow and maturity. It is the low number, the basic requirement for the fruitful Christian life. Training comes through the victory of walking through difficulty or sorrow into maturity in faith. That is how faith grows. First, it is tested then endurance has a chance to grow and become fully developed in strength of character.

> *Consider it pure joy, my brothers and sisters, whenever you face trials of many kinds because you know that the testing of your faith produces perseverance. Let perseverance finish its work so that you may be mature and complete, not lacking*

anything. James 1:2–4

The number sixty represents full circle, fullness of time, earthly king and the price. This is the next level of productivity in the Kingdom of God. The mature Christian is now in the habit of completing the cycle and mentoring others to produce fruit. They are kings on earth ruling over their circumstances, not being dominated by them. These people represent king Jesus Christ well. They have counted the cost of being a disciple. The number one hundred symbolizes the elect of God, the holy, set apart children of promise, the full number and growth cycles. This number is talking about the productivity possible through the holy children of God who love Him and know Him as Father just as Jesus did. Jesus speaks of one hundred increase, using the word "even." It is reminiscent of the way He later prophesied that we, those who follow after Him, will do "even" greater works than He.

> *"Truly I tell you, whoever believes in me will do the works I have been doing, and they will do even greater things than these, because I am going to the Father". John 14:12*

God can accomplish spiritual health and vigorous growth no matter what soil is around us. A principal of supernatural increase is: **Increase is fully available to all who live in agreement (as one) with God by His Spirit**. It seems that the four soils represent conditions everyone faces at some point in life but the progression toward healthy growth shown in the last example depends on receiving the revelation of our condition in comparison to the fertile soil. Jesus was drawing the crowd into the place of self-examination (self-focus if you will). We today still need to evaluate the true condition of our hearts. Even a small degree of hindrance will create a ceiling in our experience of God. We cannot even really know the condition of our hearts without the help of Holy Spirit.

Holy Spirit are there hindrances in my friendship with
You?

As we relax and listen to His thoughts bubbling up from
within we can repent, forgive others, and receive healing.
God will do the job of removing the blockages and pulling
away the ceiling so that you can know Him more fully.
Keep in mind that the process of knowing God is a life
long journey of continuous cleansing and restoration.

The Wheat and the Weeds (Matthew 13:24–30)

From the story of the farmer, which illustrates individual
spiritual condition, Jesus begins to talk about the
Kingdom of Heaven. This is a big picture story with which
He illustrates the spiritual condition of the earth. We
know the metaphor because later in the day He explains
it to His disciples. Why tell the story to the people using
this parable? I believe He was letting people, who were
listening in faith, know that it is because of God's mercy
and concern for His precious children that He doesn't
put a stop to evil immediately. There is purpose in God
mercifully holding back the harvest: for the sake of those
who will receive the good seed and grow in it. I believe
the good and evil seed also represent truth and lies, both
in words and ideologies.

The message Jesus taught opposed religious thinking and
popular cultural beliefs of that day. Jesus was teaching
new revelation of what God required and it clashed with
the teaching that they had heard. It seems Jesus told this
story so that people would not lose focus on God's heart.
He taught so people would know God for themselves, so
they would desire to live in relationship with Him and
would grow to love God's ways. These desires, when
activated in the human heart give birth to lives of faith

and supernatural empowerment.

The old religious teaching produced fear of punishment and the dead works of human effort. Rigid obedience to laws also seeded religious pride and self-justification. As in those times, today our focus can all too easily be diverted by high-sounding ideas and ideologies which have nothing to do with deepening our love of God. Religious ideologies have more to do with self-gratification and feeling good about how well we are doing spiritually. On the other hand, they can have the hook of obligation, guilt, or condemnation if we do not live up to them.

The Mustard Seed (Matthew 13:31–32)

This story is talking about the Kingdom of Heaven. The mustard seed symbolizes faith in God. The plant that becomes very big can symbolize the Church. In previous illustrations Jesus gave on this day, the birds represented that which snatches away truth. It seems that the birds of the air that nest in the church are those who would bring in the teaching of man and religious ideology which makes a nest among the people of God using them for their own gain.

This story was a prophetic warning that would actually become the fate of the young church in the times of the Roman Emperor, Constantine. Constantine saw the courage and faithfulness Christians displayed, under great persecution. He desired to have these attributes in his subjects. He designed the religious system to mingle Christianity with Roman Imperial ideology. This was accomplished over his reign, proving to be a great loss for Christianity, and resulting in the sons and daughters of God shedding their blood ever since. This lesson from history teaches us to keep our focus on the One who plants and not to be distracted or misled by the seductive chatter of birds who would take opportunity to make nests of heresy, or to influence us to deviate from the teachings of Jesus Christ.

The Yeast (Matthew 13:33–35)

This is another story in which Jesus shares the truth of things to come. Unleavened bread was used on holy days because it symbolized spiritual purity and holiness. The yeast bread was not set apart for special holy days. In fact, before Passover the mother of the house would go to great lengths to rid the house of all leaven, cleaning meticulously all leaven from the house. The reason for this thorough cleansing was that yeast or leaven represents sin.

The illustration was not lost on this Jewish audience. They knew Jesus was talking about the yeast (sin) of the Pharisees, which He would later tell his disciples to be careful of. Yeast like religiosity or error, spreads through out a mixture puffing it up. The analogy when applied to groups of people represents prideful thoughts or ideas that cause people to feel self-important. People then are no longer satisfied by the simplicity of following their God. Pride (spiritual or otherwise) can cause us to look to human hierarchy and systems as a way to serve ourselves. In fact, pride is the product of any mindset that would oppose the knowledge of God and the teachings of Jesus. When we lose the significance of Jesus' teaching on what pleases God, we begin the journey away from humility and childlikeness. Jesus showed us by His humble example of serving, healing, forgiving and loving even the lowest members of society.

We need to keep our hearts pure and simple before God, being content to seek His kingdom and His righteousness, and all we need will be given to us. Jesus is warning against the issue of sin and pride, which begins to affect us and those around us when we allow even a tiny amount into our human thinking and practices. Pride gets in when we cease to give attention to Jesus but instead focus on ourselves and those around us.

The Hidden Treasure (Matthew 13:44)

Jesus was talking to His Kingdom family about intimate family principals. The first four parables were for everyone present at the out-door meetings. For the lost and as yet unbelieving, for the religious unbelieving, for those who were open to His teaching and on their way to becoming family as well as for His disciples. As Jesus began to teach inside the house, he uses parables of a more personal and intimate nature which tell of passion for the most valuable treasures. These are the illustrations which speak to believing hearts about the worth of leaving every other pursuit in favour of following Jesus.

He told them that the Kingdom of heaven was like a treasure that a man discovered hidden in a field. In his excitement he hid it again, sold everything he owned to get enough money to buy the field and to get the treasure too! The symbolic meaning of the field in previous stories was explained by Jesus to be the earth and the treasure would be the precious truth of the gospel of Christ (friendship with God). I believe the man hid the treasure again inside his own heart. He did not want it to get stolen. He hid it in the soil of his heart, pondering its true value to him. Then he counted the cost to himself. The cost to him was things like his possessions, ambitions or plans for his own life. He would pay at the cost of all he owned. It would change his life and how he viewed those things significantly. However, because he judged the treasure to be most valuable he gave all he possessed to own the eternal treasure. He focused all his energy and attention to own the one thing of real value, which is actually the treasure of possessing the essence of God (Holy Spirit).

The Pearl Merchant (Matthew 13:45–46)

The pearl merchant follows a very similar theme using different metaphors to emphasize the value of the gift of eternal life in union with God. The pearl merchant is a person searching for eternal truth – one looking for God with a motive of finding the choice pearl, which is truth that is pure, precious and costly. Pearls have much significance in biblical symbolism: The gates of the New Jerusalem (gates of God's heavenly city) are made of pearl. Pearls represent purity, beauty, truth or things very precious to us. Pearls were used as currency for trade and they can be natural, cultured, fresh water or salt water.

Let's put that understanding into the context of a man who is an expert at evaluating pearls and who is seeking the very best: when he finds this one, the pearl of great price, he wisely sells everything he owns to buy it. His action makes perfect sense. How could he lose? Pearls were as valuable as money but because of their beauty and rarity they appreciate in value.

This one was "the pearl." It was the one and only, worth such a great price. This reminds me of God's one and only Son. He is beautiful, the only one who could give the gift of eternal life and the only one who loved passionately and purely enough to do it. Jesus imparts revelation of the value of sonship, being not only connected in relationship to God but of being a son. Just as God loved the world so much He gave His only son, we see the eternal value in loving God so much we give up our whole world for His life. No other thing is as precious as being one with God.

The Fishing Net (Matthew 13:47–52)

The final illustration Jesus used to teach that day was of net fishing. It was a "no brainer" for everyone. They were almost all fishermen themselves and they got it! There will be a day of sorting and those who are aligned with wickedness will perish.

Then Jesus told them

> *"Every teacher of religious law who has become a disciple in the Kingdom of Heaven is like a person who brings out of the storehouse the new teachings as well as the old." Matthew 13:52*

He has slipped in a final eighth metaphor about someone who takes new and old from the storehouse. It seems like an unrelated topic, but is relevant to the net story as we shall see. Jesus puts the order, or priority, on the new by putting it first. He purposely says the opposite to what people would normally say. Most often a comparison would be ordered with the first thing that happened in time order, but He says the new first then the old. Jesus is telling them the priority: the new will be a fulfillment of the old, just as He fulfills the Old Testament pictures and prophesies. The teaching He is giving is the fulfillment of the law. We see in Jesus the fulfillment of the law, so that the law would be written on our hearts by the Holy Spirit's promptings. Relationship with God has replaced the arbitrary legalistic living of the Pharisees. The old teachings were delivered to guide people to God to keep them from harm, and they remain as the signposts on the well-traveled road of spiritual life. The Old Testament teachings cannot empower us to go beyond, to do the things Jesus did.

As Jesus was careful to say, "every teacher of religious law who has become a disciple of the Kingdom of heaven will have access to understanding the new (which He just introduced in the net story) and the old. The new concept of the harvest of mankind, judgment and punishment based on righteousness, is foundational to understanding. No one is good enough to be called righteous without the Saviour. Jesus was teaching them where their focus needed to be on the new teaching which the old confirms. If we focus on Old Testament teaching we can become stuck in the old order of the priesthood and the law that was only given as a sign pointing to the liberator, Jesus Christ.

Balance comes as the disciple of Christ draws from His teaching using the historical books of Scripture as the ground floor. History serves as a foundation for the New Testament teachings of Jesus and the Apostles. The reason Jesus specifically states "the teacher who is a disciple in the Kingdom of Heaven", is because those who were still only relying on the religious law would not accept the radically opposing concepts of the Kingdom.

In our day one would hope believers focus on "the new" Jesus alludes to, but sadly, many have not understood the Kingdom message of grace that Jesus taught. Their focus is on trying to live according to rules of behaviour, instead of living from grace and empowerment given to us by the Spirit of Christ.

5 – Living Life

Contemplating Jesus "the Life" is the most productive use of our time here on earth. Any soul will change for the better if their faculties (mind, will, emotions, conscience and imagination) are focused on beholding Him. It does require quality and quantity time to learn the disciplines of focus and to practice them. Our customary 10-minute devotional reading, even if we do it morning, noon and night, is a pittance in light of a lifetime gain from the change in our nature God has in mind. We can have many challenges in allowing ourselves to "waste" time in this way. Our lives are packed with so many "essential" things it is hard to justify just being still before God and giving him undivided attention.

It was helpful to me as I began to change my daily routines to accommodate hours of devotion, to think of the time as an offering of love. I give offerings of money to God, so I thought of offering my time. After all, God really doesn't need my money and I gladly give it as a token of gratitude, so why not my time? Thinking of time as my love gift to Jesus gave me the permission I needed to spend hours with Him. I discovered there is always more to learn of Him, always more of God to encounter. And the best part of all, no matter how much time I give Him, my days seem to be more productive than ever. Work is accomplished with ease and in less time than usual. Peace and joy accompany me instead of the usual feelings of time pressure I would expect from having less time. In fact, I have experienced the gift of supernatural time on several occasions.

As we give attention to Jesus, His presence becomes more evident around and inside of us too. Jesus is the living word made tangible on earth for a short time in history. Now He has come again to rule and reign in us, by His Spirit. Now the supernatural presence of Christ is tangible to our supernatural senses, just as He was once tangible to the natural senses two centuries ago. Our kinship in His family is secured by His blood covenant, so we can know God intimately as we would a best friend, a parent or a marriage partner. The Holy One has come to dwell within and among us. We can sense His companionship, if we choose to turn our attention to Him.

Following Jesus is as simple as including Him in our internal conversations. Including God the Spirit in every moment of our day is a practice not natural and humanly quite impossible. However, it is entirely desirable, accomplished by His Spirit's power working in our yielded heart. All we need is the willingness to ask God to begin the process. He will give the hunger and opportunities.

Down through the centuries, people we now call Mystics longed for and attained the realized presence of Jesus Christ in their every day life. These were ordinary people with a passionate desire, willingness to yield, and faith that God would meet them. People just like you and me – people willing to take the journey into loving God with all their heart, soul, mind, and strength. They were not disappointed and are among the great cloud of witnesses in Heaven, watching us, encouraging us by their examples, to live in supernatural encounter every day, as they did.

As we yield and choose to turn our affections toward Him, Jesus draws us near into the delightful experience of the joy of His company. Along the way we will also experience all the benefits of His kingdom.

But seek first his kingdom and his
righteousness, and all these things will be
given to you as well. Matthew 6:33

Listening Prayer/Meditation Exercise
Jesus please speak to me about living in union with You?

Book 2: The Truth

Priceless Pearl

Jesus talked about pearls, as we have seen in the first book, in the parable of the pearl merchant. He also warned not to throw our precious pearls to those who would not value them.

Pearls are such a wonder of nature, a picture of the beauty and purity of truth. The oyster forms them through the process of coping with an irritation. A little piece of sharp-edged grit that gets inside its shell irritates the flesh of the oyster. Imagine, something so beautiful being a reaction to something annoying! That beautiful coating of the mother-of-pearl is what draws us to want to own such a treasure. I'm sure no one would want the rough little rocks and bits that were their beginnings. It would be very odd indeed to spend what we do on pearls for such ugly, rough things. I think pearls make a wonderful metaphor for several spiritual truths worth our pondering.

- Pearls can be formed from the hardest, most annoying, even painful things in our lives. These treasures come through the work of Holy Spirit, our "Mother-of-Pearl", working grace and mercy over and over, coating our wounds and trials to create patient endurance and deeper appreciation for God's truth. Pearls are the grace evident through someone who has learned to come to God with everything. Allowing His redemptive work to coat and mould us will bring beauty, even in the hardest things life has given us. That redemption causes others to notice and want the same.

- Truth can be the grit that is hard to accept, that annoys our flesh, and that gets our attention so that we must face the fact it presents. If we allow truth into the depths of our soul (through our shell), it will penetrate our flesh, and do its work. Then truth will become the beauty of our lives. The pain of corrective truth works deeply to change and free us to live in the beauty of God's holiness.

- When we have undergone the deep work of redemptive truth and aligned our healed hearts, we become the pearl. We will carry truth wrapped in grace and mercy. As people are ministered to by grace and the pure kindness of mercy, the truth will be seen as the gift it is intended to be. Others will be moved to take hold and possess this good gift – the pearl of truth.

The Foundation

More than any other relationship, this one of us and God, must be based on truth. The truth about ourselves, God and others produces healthy thinking. If we want to grow in the knowledge and love of God (which is His desire for us) we must be honest, real, and vulnerable with Him. We cannot hide from the lover of our souls, nor would we want to when we understand His love. It takes humble admission and often repentance to bring us into agreement with God's perspective.

Spiritual realities which are shared in this portion of "Divine Focus" are helpful in understanding how unchanging truth works to shape our lives. We will examine what is to be gained from yielding to truth. As we noticed in the pearl analogy, truth can be irritating to our flesh, but as is often said these days: "No pain no gain! That truth was very evident in the life of Jesus Christ. He, who is Life, gave up life for the sake of giving life to us.

1 – Grace and Truth

In the beginning God spoke and things formed from nothing. The living word creates life from nothing. God's breath in those first words caused life to manifest. Jesus Christ is life and is full of grace and truth. It must have been glorious to experience Jesus, the Word incarnate, living among ordinary messed up people.

> *The Word became flesh and made his dwelling among us. We have seen his glory, the glory of the one and only Son, who came from the Father, full of grace and truth.*
>
> *John testified concerning him. He cried out, saying, "This is the one I spoke about when I said, 'He who comes after me has surpassed me because he was before me". Out of his fullness we have all received grace in place of grace already given. For the law was given through Moses; grace and truth came through Jesus Christ. No one has ever seen God, but the one and only Son, who is himself God and is in closest relationship with the Father, has made him known. John 1:14–18*

There was a word from God given through Moses. It was the word of God, but not the fullness of His word. The fullness would come through Jesus and it would be wrapped in grace. The law does not contain the fullness of grace, though it was a measure of it. God wanted to save mankind from the depravity we would reach without His intervention. Through the law God was telling mankind how far was too far, in clear cause and effect terms. Breaking the law is unhealthy to say the least, had terrible consequences and was punished. The law is a kind of societal safety net to catch us before we are destroyed by sin. So, the law is a gracious gift from God that has helped us but, is not equal to what Jesus came to demonstrate. Grace and truth seem to be such opposite concepts, yet were united and brought to us in Jesus Christ. The balance of grace and truth in the life of Christ has freed us from captivity to the law of sin and death.

Books and sermons have been given on the topic of grace, yet a diversity of opinions has created controversy around this topic. Fear of people taking grace too far, living an unbridled life without consequences, has been reason enough for some teachers to voice grave concern, even though the Apostle Paul addressed it. He made it clear that more sin is an abuse of the grace of forgiveness. Still, there are those who have fears that teaching people God's exceptional, unconditional grace will give the green light to sinful living with no fear of punishment. The opposite actually seems to happen, especially to Christians. We tend to be more prone to accept guilt and condemnation under legalistic thinking rather than the grace of God's forgiveness when we fall.

Twin Aspects of Grace

It has been said that grace is the good will of God toward us (the first aspect), and it is the good work of God in and through us (the second aspect).

Toward us: We can think of God's grace as unmerited favour, being accepted by God no matter how undeserving we are.

In Us: Grace is the divine influence on a life, which

endows special strength and ability to act beyond what is natural. This aspect of grace is reflected in the outward life of the recipient. Combining these aspects together, we can see that:

Grace is a generous free gift from our Creator that brings freedom from legalistic living, joy in following God's desire and supernatural ease with which to live by God's power in life.

As alluded to previously, truth is incarnated through Jesus Christ. He is the personification of truth. In other words, if you could see truth lived out, Jesus is it and more. Truth definitely has a point to it.

> *For the word of God is alive and active.*
> *Sharper than any double-edged sword, it*
> *penetrates even to dividing soul and spirit,*
> *joints and marrow; it judges the thoughts*
> *and attitudes of the heart. Hebrews 4:12*

That is the thing about the word of God (truth). It has the capacity to bring separation of the soul and spirit which, is hard to take. However, Jesus Christ is the union of grace and truth. He did not water down truth in order to be gracious. When infused with grace, truth has an even better penetration into the human heart. Grace is like oil on truth that helps people to receive the lancing effect truth has. Truth sets us free, but it can cause us to feel accused, which will cause us to protect our hearts or hide from the exposure of our faults. Grace pours love and acceptance on our flawed human condition and offers, in advance, the pain reliever, which makes the lancing of truth bearable.

Truth Married Grace

We need the demonstration of God's grace intertwined with the truth of the law. Grace alone, without the penetration of truth, would not bring correction when needed. Lives are ruined when lived without the guidance of absolutes. Much harm has come from the anarchy of relativism and situational ethics in our society today. On the other hand, truth without grace gives only bare facts, possibly leading us back to living from rules with no freedom to evaluate exceptions. God gave the solution to mankind's alienation from Him by sending the perfect marriage of grace and truth in human form. We desperately need to live in this marriage. We live in this marriage by living in union with God. This is the perfect union that our lives are created to consummate.

Something precious we see when studying the life of Jesus is the intimate, vital, daily, relationship He had with God the Father. This was a radically different life than following law. If we live like Jesus, abiding in God, our attitudes and behaviours will be modified into the beautiful combination of grace and truth Jesus had. In fact, Jesus is the book written in human flesh, the manual of how truth mingled with grace looks. We can see from His life that He didn't come to give a new way to live by the law. He didn't come "to do away with" the law. He fulfilled the Mosaic Law and satisfied its demands so we wouldn't have to. Jesus demonstrated a much higher life than the low bar of law. The truth is, mankind couldn't fulfill even the low requirements of the Mosaic Law so, how on earth could we fulfill the higher standard Jesus gave when He said:

> *"Do not think that I have come to abolish the Law or the Prophets; I have not come to abolish them but to fulfill them. For truly I tell you, until heaven and earth disappear, not the smallest letter, not the least stroke of a pen, will by any means disappear from the Law until everything is accomplished. Therefore, anyone who sets aside one of the least of these commands and teaches*

*others accordingly will be called least in the
kingdom of heaven, but whoever practices
and teaches these commands will be called
great in the kingdom of heaven. For I tell
you that unless your righteousness surpasses
that of the Pharisees and the teachers of the
law, you will certainly not enter the kingdom
of heaven.*

*"You have heard that it was said to the
people long ago, 'You shall not murder,
and anyone who murders will be subject to
judgment.' But I tell you that anyone who is
angry with a brother or sister will be subject
to judgment. Matthew 5:17–30*

Over and over Jesus set people free from condemnation
and judgment that legalism was enforcing. He broke
protocol to give mercy, forgiving those who were worthy
of punishment by the law's standards. Ultimately, He was
ostracized by leaders, and took the brunt of their offence
at His acts of grace toward sinners. Mercy, through Jesus,
radically triumphed over judgment. It was not popular
then and still it seems that grace is misunderstood today.

Truth needs grace and grace needs truth to exemplify the
beauty of Jesus life. Neither grace nor truth can be altered
for if we try to soften truth or sharpen grace we will lose
their ability to set us free. When we grasp that they are
complementary concepts, and receive them together we
are free from condemnation and shame to come to God
just as we are. We can come when we are in the mess of
sin and self-loathing, just as easily as we can come when
we feel good about ourselves. We are welcomed to enter
into the Fathers love in every moment of life.

Don't Miss the Moment

Though it is difficult to come to the Father when we have a heavy conscience, we especially need to come to God then. We need Him even more when we feel condemned or unworthy. Those times are teachable moments for our heavenly parent. He is the antidote for shame and condemnation. He desires to help us find truth and grace to go deeper. His desire is to teach us, not through punishment but through His lavish love. Forgiveness and grace are His gift, and will in turn, be ours to give others. Remember, vengeance and punishment belong to the law. God wants to love us even in our most wretched moments – especially then. The problem of our human thinking is that we just don't understand His amazing grace. So, here is the dilemma: God wants to forgive but we think our misdeeds "need" to be punished. No one would choose to whip themselves, would they? Oh yes, they do! In fact, we all have. I have punished myself by not coming to God, by hiding till I had sufficiently repented and beaten myself up for failing (yet again). All the time we are self-flagellating, Jesus patiently waits. He wants us to just thank Him for what he has already done. He would like us to move on with Him into who he designed us to be.

> *I have been crucified with Christ and I no longer live, but Christ lives in me. The life I now live in the body, I live by faith in the Son of God, who loved me and gave himself for me. Galatians 2:20*

You see, our identity is rooted in Christ. His identity is revealed through me. Jesus is waiting to be revealed to all creation through His children (us). I am already crucified with Him so why do I try to kill myself again with every mistake I make. If I am living by faith, even though my flesh messes up, I am still seated in Him and am forgiven. The process becomes a one step forward and two steps back if I keep forgetting the grace and truth of the gospel. I am applying the law of sin and death to myself when I try in human effort to live by rules and punishment. The concept of life-giving grace and truth has been examined well by our brother Apostle Paul.

> *Therefore, there is now no condemnation for those who are in Christ Jesus, because through Christ Jesus the law of the Spirit who gives life has set you free from the law of sin and death. For what the law was powerless to do because it was weakened by the flesh God did by sending his own Son in the likeness of sinful flesh to be a sin offering. And so he condemned sin in the flesh, in order that the righteous requirement of the law might be fully met in us, who do not live according to the flesh but according to the Spirit. Romans 8:1–4*

Focusing on my sinful inadequacy takes my attention from His sufficiency. Living in regret and condemnation takes me into a negative mindset that limits me to mere humanity. My real identity in Christ, fused to His divinity makes me a son of God and as such, I am always welcome to come to my Father. Even the prodigal came back, so can I. That father of the son who disgraced himself and wasted his inheritance, waited, longing for his sons return. God is waiting, always ready to embrace and renew covenant with us because He has provided grace with the truth in Jesus.

> *All of us also lived among them at one time, gratifying the cravings of our flesh and following its desires and thoughts. Like the rest, we were by nature deserving of wrath. But because of his great love for us, God, who is rich in mercy, made us alive with Christ even when we were dead in transgressions—it is by grace you have been saved. And God raised us up with Christ and*

*seated us with him in the heavenly realms
in Christ Jesus, in order that in the coming
ages he might show the incomparable riches
of his grace, expressed in his kindness to us
in Christ Jesus. For it is by grace you have
been saved, through faith—and this is not
from yourselves, it is the gift of God— not
by works, so that no one can boast. For we
are God's handiwork, created in Christ Jesus
to do good works, which God prepared in
advance for us to do. Ephesians 2:3–10*

The Father has taken us into His family. We are seated
with Him in Christ. No matter what happens we are
already positioned in Him. We have grace in our time of
weakness. We are freed by the truth of His approval. Not
that our misdeeds and shortcomings earn His approval
but because of His amazing grace we are loved and there
is no separation between us. The blood of Christ has dealt
with sin and separation. Now we are positioned in truth
by His grace. Actually, we don't have to understand it. Our
only need is to receive God's grace and truth together. The
combination defies human reasoning. When we feel we
need to be punished, He surprises us by loving us to life,
through His grace and truth. Our part is to remember who
we are, accept the truth of His approval of us and allow
His grace to be our sufficiency. We can be set free by His
truth – that which must define us, not our performance.

Listening Prayer/Meditation Exercise
On that note take a moment to contemplate the words of
this old Hymn.

Ask yourself: "Will I once and for all believe and receive
the truth of grace?"

"Grace Greater than Our Sin"
Julia H. Johnston

Marvellous grace of our loving Lord,
Grace that exceeds our sin and our guilt!
Yonder on Calvary's mount outpoured,
There where the blood of the Lamb was spilt.
Grace, grace, God's grace,
Grace that will pardon and cleanse within;
Grace, grace, God's grace,
Grace that is greater than all our sin!
Marvellous, infinite, matchless grace,
Freely bestowed on all who believe!
Look! There is flowing a crimson tide;
Will you this moment His grace receive?

2 – Hunger

There is, in every soul, a longing for connection with the divine source. There is desire for absolute and complete belonging. Most of us struggle to find ways to quell this longing. Many of us feel a deeply buried loneliness, an ache that says, "I'm not quite whole, something is lacking in me." Beginning in infancy, a child cries out because they ache. Depending on the circumstances, the child may to some degree be comforted. In every case the longing is not just a want; it is a need that drives to be met. Like physical hunger where discomfort accompanies the need, soul hunger is also uncomfortable, even painful.

This basic drive for food compels us to act. We must eat something! It is life and death. Though we may want a certain food, if there is no choice anything available will do. The pain of hunger will compel us to meet the need. Every parent has experienced the demanding cries of a hungry baby that are not at all easy to ignore and for good reason.

In good circumstances, a child will be fed and loved by parents who may not be perfect but do have loving intent. For some children however, this is not the case; the basic needs are not lovingly filled. The urgency of hunger for food, as well as the need for attention, affection and human care become intense to the point of desperation. Need is intensified by lack, and even worse, abuse.

Whether, as children, we are treated with human

kindness or not, we all experience soul hunger in varying degrees. Connection to God, who is our source of spiritual food, gives our souls satisfaction. Sustenance comes as we draw on God's supply of unconditional love and acceptance. Only that substance can truly satisfy. The longer we live without this spiritual food, the more intense our soul's need becomes.

Amazingly, after a while, a baby can adapt to neglect. It will suffer many different issues that ultimately prevent it from thriving, but strangely, it will stop the incessant screaming. It is not that the child is no longer hungry, lonely or in need of a new diaper but, it copes with the lack of care by adjusting to the discomfort. Hopelessness is not without negative effect, but when it sets-in, the child accepts that his or her needs will not be met by crying. Sad to say, a child goes into a place of utter resignation. As a child grows, it begins to meet its own needs, though it may choose very poorly and suffer malnutrition. As soon as it can get to something edible it will eat. Likewise, a child will work at getting emotional needs met the same way. Attention, or any kind of affection, drives the child too often to negative or harmful placebos.

> *Hope deferred makes the heart sick, but a longing fulfilled is a tree of life. Proverbs 13:12*

With its need for love, acceptance and significance, the human soul begins to grab at anything to try to fill that empty place. In our soul hunger we reach out to people, to possessions, to accomplishments as well as power over others. These are attempts to fill the hunger that only God can fill perfectly. These attempts ease the emptiness for a time but, like eating junk food, it doesn't feed our bodies. We crave these things, which are addicting and cause demands of their own. This kind of temporary fix is not what we are created for. Original design has a much higher purpose than just to get a fix and limp on to the finish line. God's intention was to pour out the perfect soul food and lavish us with more that we can contain.

God's Hunger

God is love, and love also has a longing, a hunger if you will, to find a place of expression. We, His crowning creation, are the place in which that expression finds rest. The Bible tells us:

> God is light, and there is no darkness in him at all. 1 John 1:5

In other words, God is pure. God has pure motives in His love. God is longing to express this pure, unconditional love to those who will receive it. He gives His essence, His love, to all. His intention is that we take and eat this lavish, satisfying, and rich love. He is the perfect, pure, holy lover of our souls. His motive is love. In fact, God is the manifestation of love itself. Love's desire is to pour out on someone. Love's passion is to draw someone near and be joined by reciprocation. God wants to love and be loved. Jesus put it this way, that He would come and commune as a close friend if we would open the door of connection (communion) to Him.

> Here I am! I stand at the door and knock. If anyone hears my voice and opens the door, I will come in and eat with that person, and they with me. Revelation 3:20.

The choice is ours to open the door. God is right there close and waiting for our permission. To actively eat and drink of our creator is to renew our life, for in Him is all life and wholeness.

> For in him we live and move and exist. As some of your own poets have said, "We are his offspring." Acts 17:28

Divine Ingredients

There is no life outside of God. Spiritual life is sparked, as we choose to open the door and allow communion with God. A covenant is enacted when we invite Jesus, the royal guest, into our lives. The covenant is made by the Godhead. This binding agreement was the Father's design. It was Jesus passion to fulfill the requirements of the blood payment. The Spirit of God sealed the bond. We are now able, if we choose, to become one with God through a living, life- giving union.

The union of God and man first took place in the womb of Mary. The incarnation of Jesus Christ was not His conception. Jesus was in eternity with the father and agreed to be the blood atonement or sacrifice willingly for our sake. The only acceptable blood payment that fulfills the requirements of God's holy and just law is that of the sinless Son of God. Jesus is the only one who could pay for humanities sins, because He is God and man, united in one. This union, fulfilling the divine longing of God and the need of mankind, is consummated in the sacrificial love gift of Jesus Christ on the cross.

Our inner longing, the loneliness, is for God. Only God can satisfy. When the angel told Mary God's purpose for her; to become the bearer of the holy seed, she accepted her assignment with such joy. It's hard to believe how she could have been so willing when we consider the risk she faced as a single pregnant woman in those times. Yet there was such a heart within her, she knew her destiny was being fulfilled. She pondered these things in her heart. She carried this divine seed and gave birth to the Christ who is the hope of all mankind. I believe we share this destiny with Mary. As we invite the divine seed, Holy Spirit to over shadow us. He implants His essence into our human spirit. The Spirit changes our nature so we can become like Jesus Christ. We share one body with Him as His spirit dwells and conforms us into His likeness. His divine nature is fused with our human nature. We are partakers of the divine nature, newly created beings, now the Sons of God. Just as the divine spark impregnated Mary's womb, we become pregnant with the purposes of God. At a spirit level, we are a fusion of humanity and divine essence.

Amazing as it is, God's proposal of love is often not received. The fact is there is a disconnect for many of us in that we may be unaware of the overtures of divine love. Often, we are not in touch with the hunger in our soul's, because we are self-satisfying or easing our need with material possessions, self-gratifying behaviours and any number of poor substitutes. As with fast food, the symptoms of a constant diet of this type compound the longing and also bring on a soul sickness. Some evidence of this rampant malnutrition is rejection, low self-worth, isolation, shame, fear, guilt, regret and feelings of condemnation

Union with God is not only the answer to the original hunger, but is also the cure for every soul disease that life has inflicted. The cost for us is risk. The risk is that we must taste and see. We must try out this life. Connection is in truth so easy, yet people find it so hard. Indeed, all the hesitancy of hell seems to come when we consider opening the door to Jesus.

I used to be one of the soul-sick and lonely. Rejection and fear enjoyed my heart and abused me for many a year. The first step for me seemed so difficult, and I was faced with rejection, but I knew I was hungry. When I opened my life to God, the change was immediate and amazing. Healing of wounds took longer, but it is God's precious gift, my personal miracle. The how-to of reconnection is just as easy as a conversation with a long-lost companion, yet it is so significant that it will move heaven and change your world.

Reality has a way of shifting everything as truth sets you free. Truth, remember, is a person not just a concept

(John 14:6). Jesus is the incarnation of God who died for all our mistakes and shortcomings, sickness, and disease, mending our separation from God. We can simply thank Him and ask Him to apply His blood to our account, to cleanse us, blot out all record of wrongs against us, and give us His Spirit.

What happens next is a supernatural act: The Spirit of Christ connects to our spirit and we are now in union with Christ. Wow! A miracle of epic proportions takes place and we are accepted into the beloved. We received the divine spark of life that connects us to the flow of life from God. Like Mary we are destined for birthing the kingdom of God into this world. As we learn to tap into this flow of Holy Spirit, He continually gives to us all we need. We are fed from the never-ending supply of heavenly food. Faith, hope and love are now the soul food we are fee to eat forever. Just as Adam and Eve were told they could eat the fruit from the tree of life, you may feed on life from God always.

The journey into the wonders of life in God begins this way for us all, with a birth of spiritual new life. All heaven is glad as the Great Father announces, "Let the trumpet sound and the music play! Let everyone rejoice and celebrate for this one, this child of mine, is now found. My beloved has returned." Let's completely indulge, not just in our intellect, but immerse ourselves. Abundant life awaits with all the pleasures of knowing God. Let's not be picky eaters, but whole-heartedly feast together with Jesus Christ, our life giver.

Listening Prayer/Meditation Exercise
Lord Jesus please speak to me about spiritual hunger.

3 – Metamorphosis

This year I have been delighted to watch my little granddaughters raise Monarch butterflies. What amazing little wonders of God's handiwork butterflies are! They start so tiny, beginning as an egg. They hatch out into the tiniest caterpillar. A caterpillar is so small you can hardly see it at first. In the course of life, it moves from being the miniscule egg glued to a leaf, to the wee little eating machine, that consumes huge amounts of greenery. In fact, my family noted that during the stage when all the caterpillars were growing rapidly they could be heard, as small as they were, munching away!

In its chrysalis the caterpillar is once again stuck in place. I remember seeing them spaced so perfectly around the little netting tent the girls had used. I found out that caterpillars basically liquefy and reconstitute to become a creature that will never again be limited by the restrictions of a single place. The total transformation from egg to butterfly is truly a natural wonder that everyone, no matter how young or old, can enjoy by watching. The spiritual metaphor is just as lovely to ponder too.

Humble Beginnings

The beauty of this gossamer-winged creature bears no resemblance to its worm-like former self. It has had a new beginning, not only in appearance but also in every other aspect of its existence. The air, not the ground, is the environment for this graceful creature. The butterfly's food is now the sweet nectar, which it delicately sips from fragrant flowers. No longer will it munch endlessly on leaves it has crawled to. So different from the furry little consumer that is often thought of as a pest in the garden, butterflies by their presence, bring beauty and desirable change to their surroundings. This new creature cross-pollinates on its journey around the flowerbed, bringing life in its wake. People welcome them.

Spiritual transformation is no less amazing than metamorphosis. Our spiritual DNA is forever changed when merged with the Holy DNA of God; the old nature must die to allow the new to arise. I think that the metamorphosis of a butterfly may be more painful than scientists can measure. As a caterpillar becomes restricted by the confines of the cocoon and then liquefies, I think pain must be involved. I can tell you first hand that spiritual metamorphosis, death of human ambition, self-focus, willfulness and living for myself is very uncomfortable. We have so much to which we cling. It is painful to let go of those things that have become so dear – and yet they will surely keep us bound to the ground of human understanding munching that which is meant as food for lower creatures.

Like a metamorphic creature, the process is not in our hands to control. Spiritual recreation is supernatural. Self- effort, even though it is of good motivation, has no power to perform it. As the new spiritual nature replaces the old, the soul is completely changed so the old desires and hungers weaken in their appeal. A gradual dissatisfaction with the old life increases as revelation of the new identity, the new nature, becomes apparent. When the Spirit of Christ stirs, the soul will not look to the old things to satisfy

Through this spiritual transformation as "new creatures"

we learn to see ourselves as children of God. Life will depend upon drinking the nectar of His word and drawing on His presence. Like emerging from the darkness and restriction of the cocoon, the human soul is now fused to and completely one, with God. Not unlike a butterfly, a child of God has a new world of possibilities. No longer restricted and bound to the natural, God's children have access to spiritual realities because they are seated in the heavenly realms with their Father. The child of God is in Christ, a co-heir with Christ and has full access to all things in Him.

> *"For he raised us from the dead along with Christ and seated us with him in the heavenly realms because we are united with Christ Jesus". Ephesians 2:6*

A caterpillar has no choice in the matter of metamorphosis; it simply complies with that which is inevitable. We, on the other hand, have the choice to yield to the process, or to remain stuck in the earth-restricted human life. We can deny our Creator the pleasure of relationship and stubbornly munch the fodder of human resistance, or we can choose to agree with Him in the process and receive our wings. Painful as the cocoon may be, the pleasures of flight make the death experience of the cocoon seem such a small price. As we agree with God, He transforms our hearts, our desires and our self-image. The Holy Spirit, mingled with our spirit, begins to work in changing our nature.

The process is moved forward at an individual pace depending on our yieldedness to the promptings of the Holy Spirit. This union with the Spirit of Christ is empowered and directed by God, not a matter of our own effort to change ourselves. Our part is to give permission, as the divine nature quickens us to areas that need transformation; we agree and ask that the process be done. It is not by my effort to please, nor by self-denial or religious obedience that transformation occurs, but by the power of the living God working in me. God, the Life Giver, gives new spiritual life that causes spiritual metamorphosis. So, even though each of us must choose transformation, none of us can do it.

> So he said to me, "This is the word of the Lord to Zerubbabel: 'Not by might nor by power, but by my Spirit,' says the Lord Almighty. Zechariah 4:6

Safely Cocooned

The spiritual cocoon forms as a safe protected place. It involves time rather than a being physical place. What looks like dormancy of the cocoon state is the stillness in which we get to know God. Much must be completely changed. Even the motivations of life are liquefied to be modelled by the loving light of God. Learning to be still and receive from God is fundamental to the change needed in becoming one with God. The revelation of truth, awareness of purpose and destiny, all work inwardly to completely revolutionize the human soul. This phase is the babyhood of spiritual awakening. God is revealing Himself and in so doing our perceived identity is broadened and stretched to include new concepts. These concepts include our new identity as part of the body of Christ, becoming a son and co-heir with Christ. We also have to come to the truth that we are the temple of the Holy Spirit, a vessel containing the glory of God and we are unified with God in spirit. As the soul receives these realities, profound change occurs. Much healing is needed in order for these realities, to be fully received. The full revelation of this new self is an on-going life journey that will in Gods timing, be matured. The process of healing and maturity begins in the cocoon but is not finished there. The soul must emerge in order to live a healthy life of spiritual maturity.

The Struggle to Emerge

Emergence means risk. Like a butterfly's struggle to break from the cocoon, so we struggle with ego, our own desires, pride and judgments. The struggle is proof that inner change is taking place. The more we trust and yield our lives, the more we emerge. I believe the truth of God's unconditional love and acceptance cannot be over emphasized in this phase of development. It is imperative that we know God to be completely accepting of us in our struggles or we will become discouraged. He will free us from the wretched man that we once were and bring us into the freedom of the sons of God by His grace and truth.

The butterfly must rest and allow the new juices to flow, the wings to unfurl, to be empowered for flight and so must we. We need not by our own effort push ahead to fly, but by trusting and learning to listen to God. We must allow Him to fill us, by resting in His strength, listening to His voice, and receiving His touch. One-on-one time with our maker will not only empower flight but direct it. Spiritual transformation is like the rebirth of the butterfly; once we are born of the Spirit we will never again be satisfied gorging on the roughage of the natural realm. A new spiritual creature only finds true satisfaction in drinking the spiritual food of faith, hope and love. This nectar is of course, found in the presence of Jesus Christ. I think it is worth noting that He has been called the Rose of Sharon, and Lily of the Valley, both deliciously fragrant flowers.

A butterfly's proboscis draws nectar, like a straw, from a flower. God's presence is our flower and we access our spiritual nectar by drawing near in faith, believing. Faith is the proboscis that draws out the substance of spiritual food God desires for us. Through our love and friendship, we will receive His food of hope, love, peace, joy and many more divine gifts. Just being with God and practicing His presence feeds us His sweetness. God will share the secrets of His heart, if we will take time to listen

New Wings

Flight itself is such a wonder. Butterflies just seem to float and flutter allowing the wind to carry them. They don't seem to fight the wind but rest in it; adapting to its currents as they are carried on to new and lovely blooms. Our wings of love and trust carry us as we lean into the unction of the Holy Spirit within. His gentle nudging carries us into the plans and purposes of God. The things we learned in the cocoon have changed us so that we have supernatural tendencies, and abilities beyond human capacity.

Have you ever seen a butterfly acting like a caterpillar? I think it is actually impossible, even if it were to try. That is probably where we are so different from our dainty winged friends. Our agreement with the process of spiritual transformation has direct bearing on metamorphosis. Some people choose to stay within the perceived safety; the cocoon of human limitation; they misunderstand the process of rebirth. The thing about new life is that it has no past. New is not the old remodelled with a different coat of paint; it is a fresh start, a genesis. The old is gone, the new has begun. If we could see the beauty to come it would be so very easy, but that is the nature of faith – not to see.

Some people, though they move ahead in agreement with the process, never go on to fly. Distrusting the new wings, they remain clinging to the perceived safe place of human understanding with wings, but no faith to carry them into the new habitat of spiritual life. They believe in theory only. Faith has not taken hold perhaps, or not enough time spent in the cocoon receiving revelation of their identity. Even so, it is never too late to learn. Faith itself comes from God and perfect love drives out fear. If stuck, we need Him to loosen the glue of fear, apprehension or distrust. The Scripture tells us we only have to ask and it will be given, to seek and we will find, to knock and the door will be opened. All that is lacking will be supplied, even faith itself. Faith trusts enough to take the risk of letting go.

I'm sure when the caterpillar falls from a branch it hits the ground with a painful thud. The law of gravity keeps him down no matter how he may try. The equipment of wings has not yet been given. But once metamorphic change has taken place the law of gravity has a whole new application, one that enables, even gives him lift. Do you think He remembers his limitations as a caterpillar or delights in his liberty?

Butterfly by Nature

Spiritual metamorphosis once chosen will bring forth the butterfly; the process will require agreement with God but not human striving. God, creator and designer will see its completion because procreation of the children of God has come at great price; the blood of the covenant has been shed. God has invested heavily in your metamorphosis So, we can be sure He is in it; for your good and the satisfaction of His great loving heart. As we yield to His process we will be changed to become like the Spirit that is mingling with ours. The out-working of this union will be love, joy, peace, patience, gentleness, goodness, faithfulness, humility, and moderation. In my zeal for the transformed life I remember trying to perform these qualities with my human effort and self-discipline. It was impossible and caused me discouragement when I failed and pride when I succeeded, which is actually no success at all. I have come to realize that these characteristics are fruit of the Divine Spirit, not the product of my energy. A yielded heart will display these qualities as God's Spirit flows –

His own nature worked through me.

The gift of union with Christ births in the soul true spiritual identity. Each butterfly has his or her own beauty, and purpose. So it is with us. Try as we may, our true identity will not be unveiled until we come into agreement with the designer who made us. We are loved by God because He is love. We cannot be loved more by our effort to be lovable because we are loved before we are even born. Divine love has nothing to do with our performance, but it's about God's loving nature. Our purpose is found inside the heart of God. It is not hidden from those who choose to find themselves in Him. Our identity is open and waiting to be explored. When we draw near to God, who is the fragrance of life itself, we take on his fragrance; we will begin to emit Godly nature, Godly thoughts, and Godly ways, without striving as we just believe and yield. As we learn to discern His promptings, His voice in its many fragrances, we move into our true nature and unity with His purpose and take flight.

Listening Prayer/Meditation Exercise
Lord Jesus please speak to me about the process of metamorphosis You are taking me through. Where am I in the journey?

4 – Foxhole

Song of Songs is an amazing look at the soul's journey into union or marriage with God. There is a point in the story when the beloved, who symbolizes God, mentions to His sweetheart (the soul) that she needs to catch the foxes, the little foxes that are ruining His vineyard of love with her.

> *"You must catch the troubling foxes, those*
> *sly little foxes that hinder our relationship.*
> *For they raid our budding vineyard of love to*
> *ruin what I've planted within you. Will you*
> *catch them and remove them for me? We will*
> *do it together." Song of Songs 2:15*

What the divine Lover is saying to the soul in this passage is that we have a problem in our human nature that hinders our friendship with Him and ruins the fruit of "the Vine" (Jesus Life flowing to us) in us preventing us from flourishing into maturity.

To understand the metaphor more clearly, let's examine foxes and their habits. There are three ways in which the word Foxhole can be used:

1. A burrow of a fox (foxes' home), 2. A hole in the ground used by troops as a shelter against enemy fire or a firing point, 3. A place of refuge or concealment.

Examining the Second Definition

It's interesting to note that in the case of the military hiding place the enemy is in the perception of those in the foxhole. During war, both sides can be dug down in foxholes, each calling the other the enemy. So, protection from an enemy depends upon one's point of view. One man's enemy is another man's ally. The foxhole is a way to protect one's self from our perceived enemy.

Self-protection, when compared to God's protection, is a very poor choice in any sense, but especially when we think about spiritual things. Self-protection hides us from others whom we perceive as harmful, but it also prevents us from real connection with God. To be intimate with God we must be real. Self-protection is a foxhole of fearing others bullets – things like rejection, abandonment and attacks on self-worth. That foxhole is not helpful to our relationship with God, and blocks intimacy with people as well. The strategy we used for refuge becomes the prison through which we spectate, unable to enter into intimate relationships. Our refuge has entrapped us.

The First Definition

Then there is the foxhole that is the home of foxes. This is actually quite similar to the meaning of military foxholes in that it is a protective place from which to operate. Foxes do move from their dens with military-like strategy to capture their prey. Notice the metaphor in the Scripture: "little foxes". When foxes make their dens or foxholes, they often go quite close to human habitation. They are after livestock or small animals to feed on. Foxes are more active during the whelping season, with new mouths to feed. The young also damage the land and environment as they grow. Foxes bury extra or left-over carcasses which again disrupts and destroys plantings. The little foxes, though they seem small to us, are even more damaging than the more obvious larger ones that steal from the chicken coop and barn. The offspring are more numerous and so, more damaging.

Spiritual Vineyard

As we ponder the metaphor of "little foxes' and apply it to the issues of the soul's journey to maturity, we can see how human attributes, without divine influence, can be subtly ungodly. Things that are self-centred, or egocentric, like self-protection, selfish ambition and self-determination, will definitely work against God's plan for us. They are the products of self-focus. God's desire for self-less living and unconditional loving of others is ruined by the *little foxes*. These are foxes of selfish ambition, territorialism, comparison, judgment, the need for human affirmation, and human control among other issues, that ruin the soil of our vineyard. They are the little foxes that pollute the vineyard Holy Spirit is planting and prevent His work from taking root. These negative traits separate us from divine fruitfulness.

Love, joy, peace, gentleness, goodness, patience, kindness, faithfulness and moderation, are the fruit of the Holy Spirit at work in us. The production of this fruit is hindered when the little foxes are rampant. Focus on self redirects our energy and attention to meeting our own needs and protecting our interests. These needs and interests we try to meet by orchestrating or controlling our lives have actually already been met by God. Our striving will not satisfy what is already available. When we look to our own human resources, and try to meet them we turn away from the one place where these things are actually accessed. God the Spirit is in us.

True Freedom

Shifting our focus from self to God is not natural to us. It actually goes against our human nature to turn from self. The difficulty comes from many areas and is humanly quite hard, if not impossible, to surmount. Much anxiety comes from past experiences, where we have been shot at and wounded by "frenemies". The self-protect instinct is often quite strong. The need to control or manipulate may come as second nature (even first response). Sometimes the protector of self has many locks that, with the help of trained prayerful people, can be unlocked. Receiving help, like Inner-healing ministry, will give us the ability to trust God at a deeper level so that we are no longer gripped with self-protection. We can be confident that our Maker has made the way out of the prison protecting us. He knows the cause of our trust issues. He will, through the renewal that comes by way repentance and forgiveness, restore us with truth, and completely set us free.

The process of restoring the soul is worth the time it takes. Being free to hear God more clearly and to follow the Spirit of God is the most wonderful gift available to everyone who belongs to the family of God. Letting go of self-focus involves turning to God through a lifestyle of listening, then yielding to Holy Spirit. He is the lover of our soul and is relentless in His pursuit of deeper relationship with us.

Notice, the Scripture quoted the lover as saying that He will do the catching and removing of the little foxes from our vineyard *with us*. As we co-operate with God, allowing Him to show us our flaws in character, God together with us, rids our soul of hindrances. He does the work of freeing. Our part is to allow God to work – to give him the time and permission to work. He will tend our vineyard and purge us of the troubling deceptive issues. By His blood, Jesus has set us free from our human sin condition. Holy Spirit has come with the power to live an overcoming life in union with Him. Self is no longer our ruler as it was crucified with Jesus Christ. We can be freed from every fox that would ruin our vineyard. Our soul is now cultivated for the purpose of God's divine nature, His fruit to flourish in us. As the Scripture asks: "Will you catch and remove them (the foxes) for Me? We will do it together."

Listening Prayer/Meditation Exercise

Jesus please speak to me about "little Foxes" have I nurtured that undermine my true identity?

Lord please show me the root of any Foxhole of self-protection in my life.

What truth replaces these the lie that causes me to hide?

5 – Simplicity

Many of us long for a simpler life. We hear the sayings like, "Take time to smell the roses", "If we could just turn back the clock to a simpler time", "Less is more", but are these sayings true? This idyllic life we think we should wish for is often the opposite of what our ego wants.

Keeping busy feels important and successful. Full schedules, with several meetings per day, give the sense of excitement to life. We feel useful that the world needs us, though we may not actually be productive, rushing from one appointment to another. Being busy carries the illusion of accomplishment. Twenty-first Century society tells us we are "somebody" if our agenda books are filled. An over-full schedule gives a boost to our self-worth. We often evaluate other people based on their many "irons-in-the-fire". People who have a whole lot going on, though they may lack peace, are thought to be successful by the world's standards.

When we consider the alternative to this rushed and complicated life, being less busy, having time to think, actually feels uncomfortable – not because it is not good for us to have time to enjoy living life, but because we feel so unimportant when we have time on our hands. Being busy not only gives the illusion of success, but the adrenaline rush is exhilarating too. When we are in overdrive, our adrenal gland gives us an addictive boost, a high that can drop into depressed feelings if we slow down. We want so desperately to be important, to be noticed, to make our mark in the world, so we live life in overdrive. That is where the issue truly lies.

Notice the focus is on what *we* desire, what makes *us* feel important, and how *we* will look to others. It is pretty obvious where we have placed the attention. We could just stop and think about what is important. But that's the problem, we often don't think about it. We just keep doing it! We do life without taking a breather to consider how our harried, rushed pace affects our God given purpose or destiny. Self-focus will not deliver God's good and perfect will. The opposite is actually true.

> *"Jesus said if we seek first His kingdom and His righteousness all things will be added to us." Matthew 6:33*

He was talking about the things that drove society of that day. I think His admonition applies to the divineness of our day.

Besides the ego's lack of motivation to change, it takes a lot of effort to shift our focus. We probably would not initiate change until our human resources run low. Our health and relationships may demand change. It is truly God's kindness when He convicts us of our hamster-wheel life style and applies His brakes. Complicated lives take a whole lot of initiative to reset – and most of us, though we are panting for a break, really are afraid of keeping things simple.

In fact, simplicity does not mean inactivity, or having no impact with your life. It has been said that *simplicity is about subtracting the obvious and adding the meaningful*! There is a difference between the obvious (urgent "in your face" things) and the things God says are important. Eternal success is not measured by human striving; it cannot be arrived at in our own strength. Often God's successes are almost unnoticed by human eyes. A driven life will never accomplish it. It is a God focused life we must aim for. Only He can bring us to a meaningful destination.

The Minimalist Movement

A few people go to the lengths it takes to achieve a more simplified life. The minimalist movement is a reaction to our overly materialistic culture. Extreme minimalists have few possessions that their homes or should I say living spaces (for most do not believe in having much, if any, home) resemble that of a monastery cell. Imagine a place with just one chair one pillow, one plate, one pot and one set of cutlery (two if you are married). Not my idea of a cozy spot to hang one's hat (that would require a hook too). Minimalists use their electronic devices to replace anything like books and record keeping. Though their choices can be extreme minimalists say they have discovered such amazing freedom from the tyranny of caring for stuff. They do not have to earn as much to buy things, so they have more time to travel or pursue other interests – obviously not shopping!

Though the human spirit can be unaffected by material possessions, often the extreme opposites (materialistic hording verses minimalism) can be a symptom of issues of the soul (mind, will, emotions, conscience and imagination). Issues such as a poverty mindset, selfish ambition, perfectionism and greed etc., cause us to place too much emphasis on the accumulation or eradication of possessions.

Decluttering the Mind

The concept of minimalism, if not taken to the extreme, can be helpful when applied to our inner lives. When I'm in a cluttered environment (as well as it being harder for me to find things) I notice my focus on a task drifts and it is harder for me to think clearly. I become overwhelmed by the visual information around me. Similarly, when music with vocals fill the environment my ability to do mental work (write, read or process detailed thoughts) is hindered. On the other hand, if the area where I choose to work is quiet and reasonably tidy I'm freed to cognitively work and organize my thoughts. Less around me seems to create room within me to think and meditate.

Of course, there is a difference in personalities and social conditioning so that we all have different levels of tolerance to visual and audio stimulation. However, I have noted that those who make the effort to declutter their surroundings (visually and audibly) seem to find it easier to meditate on God and hear His voice. True peace and connection with God is often internal but the external has an influence on being able to focus inwardly.

Becoming Child-like

Simplicity is what Jesus talked about when He taught about coming to God as little children [3].

> *He called a little child to him and placed the child among them and he said: "Truly I tell you, unless you change and become like little children, you will never enter the kingdom of heaven. Therefore, whoever takes the lowly position of this child is the greatest in the kingdom of heaven. Matthew 18:2–4*

It is the child-like who can keep life basic, who look at life without devious motivations. When children are very young they really don't have the ability to lie or keep secrets; they are just as you see them, and proud of it! Very young children believe what you tell them. I just love the response when they are told how sweet and precious they are. "Yes. I know!" they say, without any hint of pride or arrogance. It's so wonderful to be innocent and truthful. Children are wonderfully oblivious to any sense self-consciousness.

We can choose to see life the way children do, even though as adults we have to manage the complications of life. We need to realize being authentic is a key to simplifying life. Being truly ourselves is much easier than trying to be someone we are not. As we drop pretence it may cause us to feel vulnerable, but as uncomfortable as it is, life becomes much less work. We are given permission by God to be who we are created to be

> *"You were taught, with regard to your former way of life, to put off your old self, which is being corrupted by its deceitful desires; to be made new in the attitude of your minds; and to put on the new self, created to be like God in true righteousness and holiness. Therefore, each of you must put off falsehood and speak truthfully to your neighbour, for we are all members of one body." Ephesians 4:22–25.*

The spark of who we really are is hidden under layers of insecurity, inferiority and self-consciousness, all of which make things much more work. When we choose to put off the old nature with all its pretence we are free to be real. Sometimes we need healing from emotional damage inflicted on us and our self-protecting habits. God is very intentional about bringing us out of lies we have come to believe about our identity, if we will choose to spend time hearing His truth and applying it.

Simply Love

Being with people who do not honour who we truly are can cause us to perform for them or conversely cause us to fight for identity to be acknowledged. These kinds of relationships are much more work than being in relationships in which we can be authentic. Though it takes change, we need to stop the pretence and get down to being real. Allowing the people in our lives to get to know us as we truly are is a risk that allows God to show us the true foundation of the relationship. He will give wisdom and grace to live simply as ourselves.

Healthy relationships are in constant change as people grow emotionally and spiritually. Change happens whether we want it or not. We must respond to the changes in direction and connections not clinging too tightly to others, allowing for their growth, just as we need them to give us freedom to mature. Even in life long covenant relationships like marriage, illness, death or separation can change status. God is the only stable one to cling to. The love God has is unchanging, eternal, unconditional and unlimited. Relationship with Him gives the foundation to every other relationship so that we are grounded. The stability of the love of God gives us security and contentment. God simply *is* love. He will not change His mind, become bored or drop us for another. We can find stability and peace in simply receiving His pure love.

The Beauty of Less

There have been times when I have been taken into simplicity through circumstances beyond my control. Those were difficult times of illness, relocation and times of isolation when life was bare – with less people and activities. God worked those days, months and years together for my good. I learned the beauty of less. Less energy showed me how much I had been striving. Fewer people in my life caused me to view my family with greater appreciation. I had not previously appreciated the fact that my husband and children are part of the body of Jesus Christ and as such are also the church.

Loneliness for friends and family took me to a depth in

God I may not have come to. I realized how dependent I had become on people to fill my need for companionship. Through this time of separation from them God taught me to draw companionship and contentment from Him. This lesson has been a huge blessing in my life. God has given grace to live in a different way now. Instead of coming to my relationships looking to fill my needs I am free to give from a full heart, Jesus fills my needs. I have learned to drink contentment and companionship from His presence so I no longer take those things from people but can give to people instead.

I would never have chosen this level of simplicity but in His goodness, God allowed, and in fact chose it for me. He knew the long-term gain was worth the short-term pain. Now I am so thankful for those desert times of precious little. Those times have changed me so that I see the value in coming away with Him into the desert. Now there are times when I choose to simplify, to weed out the things that have begun to sprout, things He is not calling me to.

Ways to Simplify

Less in My Day Planner: Our human nature wants involvement and not to miss anything. We must choose carefully and prayerfully what to participate in (even the good is the enemy of the best). Jesus only did what He saw His Father do, so how can we enlist in things He is not showing us to do? This point (only doing what we see or hear Jesus calling us to) has been emphasized to me many times. The results of taking on projects or commitments that He did not ask me to do have shown the great importance of obeying the promptings of God. Requests come, sometimes even pressure is applied by people who have needs or wishes they think we can fill. Learn to wait and ask God. When we take the time to get God's perspective we can be firm in our no's and confident in our yes'. When our day planner is not packed full, we have time for God-encounters and spontaneous opportunities to serve others. We will also have time to fill our spiritual tank so that we have more than enough of Him to share.

People He Chooses: This is often the most difficult place to simplify. We can become overly burdened by the difficulties of others and lose sight of the fact that Jesus is there for them too. Our part is to point people to His sufficiency, not to fill their needs. When we go further than God is calling us to, we overstep our boundaries and people begin to look to us for help, instead of Jesus. Though these are wonderful people, they may be in much need. We must get our perspective from God as to our part, His part and their part. If we do not listen to God for wisdom, our lives can become crowded with relationships that will leave less time for family, meaningful friendships and the people God *is* calling you to help. We may have to let go of some relationships in order to focus energy on the relationships God wants us to nurture. We have to ask for His grace and be led by His direction.

Fewer Projects: I love to work not only with my hands but also to write, teach, counsel and create. However fulfilling the work is, work is not my purpose. We are created to love and glorify God. In that purpose we are truly satisfied. Our human nature wants to find its own fulfillment in work but our divine nature only finds fulfillment in union with Christ. We have a choice to make: To follow human desire or to follow divine desire. I learned that though it appeals to my human nature, too many projects clog my life. The divine nature and purpose God created me to live is stifled when I am over worked. I have purposed by God's grace to devote myself to what He has created me for. God enables us to seek first His kingdom and His righteousness and as we do, all these things (not the huge clutter of good things, but the best pursuits) will be added to us.

Decluttering

Years ago, I read a book on organizing a house. It really helped me declutter by simplifying one room at a time. With the use of three bags, one marked throwaway, the next store-away and the last give-away, the participant was to empty a closet in the room completely (just one closet at a time or the project becomes overwhelming). Then begin to sort the articles. Those things that are in good condition and currently being used were put back into the closet. The broken or unusable articles were put into the bag marked throw away. By now you probably get the picture: the things you were not using in this season would be put in the bag to be stored-away and the other good but not needed things went into the give-away bag for the Good Will Centre. This method worked very well for me as a mother of five living in a very modest sized home! So, how does it apply to keeping our lives simple?

Using a similar procedure, make a list to help you discern God's choices for you. Go through areas of life such as: recreational choices, regularly scheduled events, relationships and opportunities for ministry. All of these categories are valid and good. We just need to know which choices are best. Pray about each event, project or relationship, asking Holy Spirit what is your assignment. Place only what you sense Him directing to to on the appropriate list. Leave those you are not called to. Take time over the unassigned items and people, that God will fulfill and assign others to them. Doing this exercise declutters one's life and automatically frees up the day planner, making room for spontaneous opportunities as well as making room for the best choices to flourish.

Living in this simple way is somewhat akin to fasting. When we fast, we must discipline ourselves, with God's grace and help, to do without whatever we have decided to fast from. Often it is tempting and somewhat difficult to stay the course in our fast, but after several days we adjust and it becomes easier. We begin to receive the benefit and this encourages us to go on and complete the fast. When we simplify it is tempting to add things, projects and events, because it feels like not enough is happening. However, if we continue to stay the course and keep things simple we will adjust and begin to receive the benefits. Some of the benefits I've noted in living a simple life are:

- Increased focus and clarity on the things that remain.
- Time to do the work we have with excellence.
- The ability to respond to spontaneous opportunities.
- Spending time with people or on projects that God brings.
- Experiencing the peace of having time to connect with Jesus and receiving empowerment, wisdom and all the good things He has for us.

Listening Prayer/Meditation Exercise
What complicates my life?

What changes can I make to simplify?

6 – One Truth

We complicate our spirituality by embracing add-on religious ideas. A little eastern mysticism perhaps seems harmless. As a little poison is added to grain in the making of certain rat poisons, so error mixed with truth pollutes truth and poisons those who take it in. Jesus Christ is the only way to life in God. He is the bridge over the sin divide between us and God. If we mix faith in Him with faith in any other god we do not really have Him. What we do have is spiritual confusion, a mixture of truth and lies. God insists on spiritual purity and has provided one way for humanity to be reconciled. Even more wonderful than the fact that our reconciliation is a gift paid for by Jesus death on the cross is that we can be made one with Him and live in a state of constant communion with God.

We can be confident God will keep us in Him and His peace as we focus on Jesus. However, if we open ourselves up to erroneous ideas and spend our time pondering and practicing unwholesome spiritual exercises we open the door to confusion. God's enemy (ours also) is looking to hinder us and woo us away from the Lover of our soul. If we dabble in anti-biblical thinking and practices we are being spiritually unfaithful to our heavenly bridegroom Jesus Christ. We commit spiritual adultery. Those are strong words and perhaps offensive to some but truth is absolute for the Christian. If we do not truly believe Jesus is the only way we need to stop calling ourselves

Christians. After all, God does not force us to follow Jesus, we are free to choose whom we serve, but we cannot follow Jesus and another god.

> Elijah went before the people and said, "How long will you waver between two opinions? If the LORD is God, follow him; but if Baal is God, follow him." 1 Kings 18:21

The people said nothing in response to Elijah's question. My hope is that we will not waver but we will choose well, to live in agreement with God our Father and cling to Jesus Christ our only Lord. Without the Spirit of Truth, which is the Holy Spirit, it is very difficult to sort through supernatural encounters, and where light is absent, darkness quickly engulfs. Jesus talks about being pure in heart and that is the prerequisite for seeing God (Matthew 5:8). With that in mind, those who are not purely followers of Jesus Christ will not have the privilege of pure encounters. The question is what about those who are not even claiming to be followers of His way?

Spiritual Curiosity

Much curiosity and hunger is stirring in our day for spiritual experience, and many who are open are dabbling in supernatural encounters. However, it needs to be noted that God has given order and instruction that Jesus Christ is the gatekeeper; He is the only way to the Father and those who try to enter by means other than His Son are thieves and robbers (illegal in their entrance), as stated in John 10:6–10.

Those who are sons and daughters, by the blood of Jesus Christ, are seated already in heavenly realms, so they have permission to enter into His throne room and come boldly before His throne of grace. Ephesians 3:12 There is no other way to receive permission. Authentic spiritual encounter is only possible for those who have the indwelling Holy Spirit, their interpreter and guide. Warning is clear to those who would trespass; deception is very close at hand if we ignore the gatekeeper, for those who enter in by the Gate are strictly His own sheep. They hear His voice and will not be led astray by the voice of a stranger. This guarantee for knowing the true voice is only for those who know Jesus Christ. John 10:1–5

In our time we will see even more need to be plugged into our Creator for wisdom, understanding, direction and peace, all of which are readily available to anyone who will just believe, receive God's Spirit and listen to Him. Purity of heart; having only one God and relying on the Holiness of His Spirit to guide, is key to receiving truthful revelation and real encounters with the Living God.

Listening Prayer/Meditation Exercise
Lord Jesus speak to me about my dedication to You.

7 – Occupation

When people ask your occupation, do you answer with your job title? Do you mention the thing you spend most of your time doing or some enjoyable creative endeavour you love? Perhaps you would answer by giving your relationship to another person like father/mother, husband/wife of someone. When God spoke to me about occupation, He was introducing a whole new concept which, as you consider it, may answer a question you're not asking but, like me, need to.

The point God was making that morning, as I sat with cozy anticipation, coffee and journal at the ready, was to expose my soul's occupation. Now there are some things I do know: I know Jesus is vitally concerned about my soul; He died for my sake, so I could be one with Him. I am more grateful than I can adequately explain, but here it was, in pen and ink for me to puzzle over.

"I am jealous for occupancy." He said. "You have given yourself to me but I am in a tug-of-war over your devotion!" Of course, I was sorry and told Him so, but it struck me that the king of my life was saying more than I was catching.

I wrote, "Please forgive me Lord." I really meant it.

His response was immediate; "Yes, I do, again and again, but your time is limited. Not like Mine. I know you want more than this – so choose more beloved! Come to Me.

Let your need, to be occupied, be met in Me. This is another part of you I would have. For all the time spent catching up on news, being entertained and reading – you have become more world conscious. I would take you out of the world, but you keep soaking it in. This world's occupation draws your attention and focus. It mesmerizes you, to lull you away from Me and I am jealous for occupancy!"

Wow! This was a spanking! Something I've come to expect from God is loving, gentle correction. This was that, but it was not anything like the conversation I thought we'd be having. In fact this was really messing with my expectation of the usual lovely time with Him each morning. The king was speaking and the weight of His words was making me squirm!

I had to admit He was right. I mean, is He ever wrong! I just didn't realize I had strayed so far. I repented. Then pondered what I'd been missing. How could I do or not do whatever it was. It was perplexing. Thoughts began to scratch at the corners of my mind and formulate into the revelation I share with you now.

The process and choice of continual turning toward God is an occupation most difficult, not because it is laborious but because it is simple. The simple life feels like not enough. We seem to want way more in our lives than is spiritually and physically healthy for us. Just think about what most of us fill our lives with now. We are glued to electronic devices, cell phones, face time, texting and all kinds of messages that interrupt us wherever we are. This new connected life brings such complication and preoccupation that it demands the attention of all of the faculties. The mind, imagination, touch, sight and sound all resonate with it. We hardly manage to relate to people who are demanding real time and attention, let alone quiet ourselves enough to converse with God.

So, here's the thing: We live in the world now, with all its distractions and delights, but God does too. The One who has our desires and destiny tucked inside His great heart is with us right now, in this present moment. The way to connect with our destiny is to connect with the Father; the inventor of it all. The conundrum is that the lights, bells and whistles of this world distract us to the degree that even those who are passionately pursuing Jesus, turn aside and look. Not intentionally but still, whether it is by intention or not, it waylays and detours our focus.

There is a Techno song by the artist Dead Mouse that repeats the phase over and over: "Sometimes things get complicated". I do believe that Canadian guy has hit the nail-on-the-head. When things get complicated human nature, striving, stress, performance and a whole lot more kick-in. When that happens, we depart from the peace-zone where God is easily found. Living simply from God's rest allows us to sense His presence. Now is the only moment we actually have. Past is gone. Future is not here. We can only be with God (the I am) right *now*. However, that also means we *can* live with Him now! As we choose to connect in the present moment we never have to be separated. He is with us now. Here's another big thought; all the people around us are also only present now. If we could just declutter to be with them, we could enjoy relationships of much greater depth.

We gain nothing from allowing this world's clutter to penetrate our souls. There is an enemy of the kingdom of God who does gain, temporarily, from our little indulgences, distractions and worldly loves. His domain encroaches and takes its toll because the world has charmed us (the people of God). We, who are called to come out of the world, who are supposed to be distributors of the kingdom of God on earth, become mired in our enemy of distraction. We get way too complicated! When self-centred life takes over and occupies our attention, Jesus steps aside. We cannot have two occupants at once. Jesus said we cannot serve two masters when He was speaking about the love of money. I think we can apply that to our love of the world too as well as self. Looking at the technical meaning of the word occupation may add light to our subject.

The Canadian Oxford Dictionary Definition Follows

Occupation: 1. What occupies one; a means of passing one's time 2. A persons' temporary or regular employment; a business, calling or pursuit. 3. The act of occupying or state of being occupied. 4. The act of taking or holding possession of (a country district etc.) by military force. The state or time of this. 5. Tenure, occupancy (to occupy).

God was, as you can by now gather, speaking to me about the third and fourth meaning of the word "Occupation". I began to put together the true heart of what was causing me to grieve the Spirit of God. My heart and mind are not able to focus on both the world and God. Both occupy space, internal room in my soul. There is a limit to how much I can focus on at once.

Look at dictionary meaning #4: The act of taking or holding possession of (a place) by military force. We can easily see how the analogy fits our topic of spiritual focus. The occupation of Jesus Christ is exclusively glorious and radiant like light. Quite the opposite is the occupation of our hostile enemy who is darkness and evil. Either the forces of light occupy, or the forces of darkness. Both cannot fill a place at the same time. Light does not coexist and continue to shine with darkness. One occupies at the expense of the other and so it is with our souls. We have illumination or darkness, by choice or by default. If we do not choose actively to turn to God and opt for His occupation, the default will be occupation of darkness and self-centred focus. If we are filled with light (God's kingdom mindsets), darkness has no place. Light occupies, darkness fills the void or absence of light.

Multi-tasking

Often, we are unaware of the fact that there is not room for God to move in us because of preoccupation. Being previously occupied or preoccupied is rooted in the popular belief that we can manage many tasks at once, called multi-tasking. The ability to "Multi-task" is actually a myth. Research is now revealing that the brain does not multi-task. In actual fact the brain has to stop one task to focus on another. Though we learn to cope with multiple stimulations, we do not function well and our ability to produce is hampered. Productivity goes down in direct relation to the amount of multi-stimulation we allow at any one time. So, when you are trying to talk and read a text, one thing is going to win out and the other will be poorly attended to. Your brain will stop and turn its attention to that which you give priority. Then, it will return to the first task. In returning to the first task it will lose efficacy, need to use memory to recall the first task, and then have to go back to the first task again. Experts have found it is ultimately, much more efficient and a whole lot less stress to stay focused on one task at a time. So, interrupting your thoughts to answer texts and emails just slows productivity and produces more errors.

Pondering what God said about being occupied, I've realized that not only does my mind become occupied and unable to focus, but my soul's other capacities also become occupied. Stories and pictures occupy my imagination. So much so, that when I try to connect with Jesus the things I've pondered, watched and listened to clog the imagination.

I love to practice the presence of Jesus by asking Holy Spirit where He is with me. I then look with the eyes of my heart (in my imagination) and connect with Him.

In fact I have a conversation with Jesus this way every morning. Throughout the day as work I communicate with Jesus. I ask questions and His voice inside me speaks thoughts and pictures that I catch and respond to. He fully occupies me, if I give room. However, there are times when there is an overflow of stories, pictures, and thoughts that fill my imagination and mind. I am, at those times, previously occupied.

Think about this: Every capacity of the soul can suffer from occupation of an unhelpful nature. Meaning; each of our spiritual capacities, as well as natural capacities, can be occupied by information leaving little or no room for God to activate them. Some examples of how occupation affects the capacities of the soul follow:

Mind & Imagination

When the mind and imagination are occupied by self-focused or unwholesome thoughts and pictures they are busy. There is no room for pondering the things of God or engaging in communion with Him. Until the memory fades and the mind loses the vivid pictures, they will come to the fore. Of course, we can choose to stop pondering self or unwholesome things and refocus. However, the more we devote the mind and imagination to pondering negative thoughts or images, the more difficult it will be to turn our attention toward God. Many times, we need to be cleansed by repentance prayer and re-dedication to be freed from persistent imagery. This happens even when the material is wholesome. For example: Every movie will become embedded in our memory and imagination, taking space in the soul. Images can pop up into our imagination for quite some time, interfering with our connecting to God.

Emotions

Emotions take up room; they occupy space as they engage the soul. When we are occupied by joy, for example, we see everything through that lens. Even the most difficult day becomes easier when joy is occupying our soul. Conversely, when hatred occupies, it invades every thought and action. Hatred can poison our day and cause us to poison the atmosphere around us, effectively occupying our space.

Just as our natural senses can become overloaded (occupied) our spiritual senses are limited too. Spiritual senses become less able to activate when natural stimuli is occupying or overwhelming us.

Smell

A nose takes in scent one at a time, the scent may have many nuances and encompass several things but the nose gets occupied by what comes in through one inhaled breath. In fact, the sense of smell gets overwhelmed after three or four different fragrances. It must be cleansed or given some time to clear before more fragrances can be differentiated. If we already smell a fragrance in the natural, we will have a very difficult time discerning a supernatural fragrance because our sense of smell is occupied.

Touch

Though we can feel many parts of our bodies simultaneously, we interpret the stimulation through our brain, which has rapid but single focus. Many of us have taken the little trick test of soaking our hand in cold water. When the same hand is dipped in hot water it senses cold for a few moments. The sense is occupied by the first sensation. The brain interprets touch in the spiritual realm also. If there is defilement through abuse or sexual impurity, the negative memories can bring mixed messages and cause confusion and fear. In such a case, inner-healing prayer is recommended, along with re-dedication of the body and the sense of touch.

If you think about it, you could probably see all the senses are occupied when stimulation is strong or extreme. The point being, we are definitely finite beings with limited capacity, we can be full, overloaded, or occupied. Our ability to perceive God's messages can be drowned out by the noise, clutter, and confusion of the complicated atmosphere around us.

It seems as though we are porous. Our skin has holes or pores. I think our souls are porous too. We exude that which fills us. Conversely, we are susceptible to being saturated with that which surrounds us. If we are filled with the light of God we radiate light to the world. If we are empty, we soak up the world in which we are immersed. Somewhat like a sponge, if there is not enough resistance against the world, the soul that is not occupied to the full capacity with God will take in that which is all around it. We are told to be in the world, but not of the world. God's total occupation of His people ensures they will be just that.

This is the dilemma of our modern age: We exist in a world densely occupied. That occupation is not always the darkness we may associate with our enemy. For those who love God and desire close communion, the issue can be the grey areas that creep in to occupy, mesmerize and charm us. We become sedated the more we soak in the delights of the world. Our enemy can lull us into the coma of apathy, where we happily sleep under his occupation. He would have us occupied and busied with the fluff of meaningless pursuit, electronic engagement, virtual life, even seemingly harmless or good time wasters. His goal is to neutralize our destiny. He hopes the precious moments, days and years slip away so that our time on earth would come to nothing. Our enemy can induce the apathy and attitude of "everyone indulges" or a little reward or pat on the back with "veg-out" time in front of the television. Though it seems reasonable, I was reminded, God has all the time of eternity but I do not. I must choose whom to serve, God or myself.

Father is longing to take up full occupancy. Jesus is waiting for us to allow His presence and power to fill every place in our souls. Holy Spirit is calling the Bride of Christ to arise and shine for her light has come. That is the call our hearts must answer. Each time we opt for God occupation over other "fillers" we have woken up just a little more into the life in union with Jesus Christ.

Though I am not perfect in that life, my heart longs for it. The question now (the one you may not be asking, but probably need to answer) is about God's occupancy. He is actually jealous for room in your life. Will you choose His occupation?

Listening Prayer/Meditation Exercise
How do I spend my time?

What occupies my thoughts?

How do I spend my energy?

Where do my resources go?

8 – Rest

Resting from Work

Some people find it very difficult to physically rest. On holidays they get bored if there is little planned activity. Those who are doers often avoid times of inactivity, even though their bodies need rest, they feel ill at ease when not working. Often these people will make their relaxation time structured and scheduled, making leisure like work.

Work is actually good for us and does give meaning to our lives. In fact, the first thing God arranged for Adam (even before Eve was created) was to give him meaningful work; that of tending the garden. This work was not labour intensive before the fall; all they had to do was pick what they needed to eat. However, they were to master, occupy, and keep this garden. God gave work to give meaning and form to their lives. With God's authority, they were to keep watch over the garden, to tend it and keep it in order. The word "keep" is translated from the Hebrew word *shamar,* which means to guard or protect. Mankind was given meaningful work to do, tending and watching over the earth, which gave a sense of purpose to them. Work brings meaning to life, but often the true purpose of our existence is veiled to us. Our work, though it can be motivating and satisfying, is not the sole purpose for which we were created. A big clue as to the reason and purpose for our creation is revealed by the way God chose to be most noticeably present in the Genesis of mankind's days.

God's Perspective on Meaningful Life

God enjoyed the cool of each day with the family He created, walking together with Adam and Eve in the Garden of Eden. Their communication was unhindered. God's presence was most keenly noticeable to the first people as they had this pleasant time, after their work, enjoying Him. Man finds satisfaction and meaning in work, but God's pleasure is to be with us. He delights in giving us meaning through work; however, His true joy is in sharing His thoughts, companionship, and in communicating His love to us. God's desire to create living beings capable of receiving His love, with the capacity to enjoy His company, was fulfilled in Adam and Eve. God's purpose for creating us was not that we do work for Him, but that we will enjoy being with Him. That we will be recipients of His love and love Him in return. I believe God desires we have even greater fellowship with Him than Adam and Eve first had. He desires us to live in constant communion or union with Him.

God in my Garden

It was God's passion to reinstate and enhance the friendship and communication lost at the tree of the knowledge of good and evil. His great sacrifice, (the death, burial, resurrection, and ascension of Jesus Christ) made possible the reinstatement of the communion once experienced in the garden. He made this life of friendship contingent on the will of each person choosing to receive His offer of forgiveness and cleansing. The choice to be near Him is ours but we must come on His terms. It is His design that we take hold of our purpose and turn our attention toward Him. I feel God's desire for unhindered communion (common union) goes further than merely restoring us to the level of friendship the original dwellers of the garden had. God's passion is that we live in union with Him through the Holy Spirit, every moment of the day not just at the end of the workday. God would be in the garden of our soul. This is, in fact, one of the main reasons Jesus Christ gave up His life. His act of sacrifice paid not only for original sin (the disobedience of Adam and Eve) and personal sin (our own acts of disobedience), but dealt a deathblow to the sin nature, which has kept each of us from friendship with God. This garden of communion (Eden) is now open to us 24/7 as a continuous spirit to Spirit connection with God.

Hindrances to Rest

The scripture states the people of Israel did not enter His rest because of their unbelief. So, they wandered for 40 years, till a new generation who could enter into the Promised Land was born. We, who have been endowed with the Holy Spirit, are a new generation who has grace to enter boldly into God's promised rest, unhindered.

> *For we do not have a high priest who is unable to empathize with our weaknesses, but we have one who has been tempted in every way, just as we are—yet he did not sin. Let us then approach God's throne of grace with confidence, so that we may receive mercy and find grace to help us in our time of need. Hebrews 4:15–16*

Confidence or trust yields the benefits of the peace of knowing God's direction.

> *Trust in the Lord with all your heart and lean not on your own understanding; in all your ways submit to him, and he will make*

The essential ingredient we need to enter His rest is trust. We must trust that our Father is ready to give us grace and help us, that He loves us and has our best interest at heart. If we lean on our understanding, our direction will not be straight. It will lead to wandering without coming into our promised land of rest, which is found in God's directives.

There is also, in our human nature, a strong desire to preserve ourselves and create our own ambitions. We all have ideas, hopes, and dreams to which we strongly attach. These human desires often drive us to work against the good and perfect purpose God has in mind for our lives. Work is a good, God given gift however, our human nature can, at times plot, plan, strive, and scheme over and above healthy boundaries. The Garden of Eden had defined boundaries where abundance was provided. Sin expelled us, but Jesus payment invites us back to the place of peace, rest, and dependency on God's abilities.

Fear of failure or missing our destiny can also cause us to strive. Wrong perceptions of God being harsh, demanding or distant, can cause us to work too hard to try to please or appease Him. We need His loving presence daily to melt away these misconceptions. Jesus said, "Human effort accomplishes nothing. And the very words I have spoken to you are spirit and life[1]."

Living from Rest

We need to yield to God's plan and to hear what He says rather than to work at achieving our own plan and believing what seems logical and good to our minds. Our hearts need to learn to trust, as the psalmist wrote;

"Surely I have calmed and quieted my soul,

---

1   John 6:63 & 64

like a weaned child and his mother; like a weaned child is my soul within me." Psalm 131:2

A weaned child is no longer clamouring for milk as a nursing infant does. This child has learned to trust that his needs will be met and that his mother loves him. As we trust God in childlike faith He will give us rest for our souls.

Entering the rest that God would have us live in is achieved as we lay down ambitions and ideas of self-actualization in favour of focusing on God. We need to cease from human effort or striving and instead learn to flow in agreement with God. We may need healing from wrong God concepts, or fears, so that we can let go of striving. The love of God will, as we choose to be still and know him, saturate and heal us. When God heals us deeply, He up-roots lies and hurts that cause our inability to trust Him.

Once we are positioned in the place of trust, it is our work simply to turn toward God and allow Holy Spirit to lead us into His rhythm of life. This turning and submission is actually the discipline of rest. As we choose to hear God's directives, and follow His advice, we live in perfect kingdom balance, at peace with God and at peace in our souls.

The Resting Place of God

There is another aspect of rest we need to consider: That of God finding rest in our human spirits. God has been opening this concept to me. As I pondered, He introduced two places where He desires to rest.

The Individual Home of God

In each person, Jesus is seeking to rest by His Spirit. He explained it to me in this way: He wants to be at home in me, with the comforts of heaven. This happens as I yield to love, peace, purity integrity, holiness, and the other attributes of Holy Spirit. He will establish, in my inner man, His heavenly rest. These attributes are a bit like heaven's furniture. He finds comfort and rest in me, in His favourite armchair of love. God settles into His comforter of peace. He drinks from His cup of joy and delights in a good meal of His righteousness. God wants communion (common union) and worship to flourish in me, and it will as I yield to His attributes.

My spirit is the home that is cleansed and ready for His furnishings. However, the soul is the property that must be completely handed over, in order for the King of Kings to completely preside over every area and aspect of my life. Sometimes we give most, if not all of our life, so that the evidence of righteousness, peace and joy bubbles from us. At other times, we allow the entitlement of self to take over a room or two. We know when the house is not completely lived in, because our peace and joy are lacking when it comes to some areas. Righteousness is Jesus hallmark on our life. When we struggle in this area our heart becomes locked and God cannot completely fill us. The biggest issue is in recognizing our problem. The clue is the peace and joy gauge. If we worry or stress over areas of life we need some honest unlocking and house cleaning. God is already aware of the rooms where self hides. We are the ones who are deceived. The remedy is repentance and trust that God will fully manage that area of life. Trust and yieldedness to His authority, restores lost peace, joy.

The Corporate Resting Place For God

The other place of rest that He desires to fill is within His Church. As we corporately gather He desires to find a permanent home where He can dwell.

God told me His desire is not that we would host a visitation, but house and accommodate His presence permanently, corporately yielding to His ways and maintaining focus on who He is in us together. He assured me that He has brought each group together and has given each one love, peace, purity, integrity, holiness and humility (as well as many other attributes) which manifested though each gathering, in varying degrees. As His people yield, and corporately connect, by encouraging, loving, and helping each other in everyday life, we are together the body of Christ. Jesus' presence not only visits but rests in complete enjoyment, joined in perfect union.

Just as we are limited individually, and need to be connected to a community of believers, we need to form the complete body of Christ by universally becoming one with other communities. Thus, the body of Christ will be formed as one coherent dwelling place fit for the King. Together as one body we are able to be effective because we house all the gifts between us. We are complete in Him individually, but now together we can make His comfort our priority. As we are mindful of Jesus presence and His preferences, we make His home in us: His nature, character and gifts become evident among us in our individual lives, in local communities as we gather and as the world-wide body of Jesus Christ, unified on Earth.

The building of the Old Testament temple is a metaphor of this concept. King David had a desire to build God a temple (though he knew God could not be limited to a building). He desired to honour God through a physical house. This was not a bad desire however, because of his calling as a warrior, he was not suitable for that task.

David was not being chastised for the warrior calling, but it was something that could not be combined with the foundation of the symbol of God's habitation.

The job was given to Solomon, who, even though he was the product of David's affair with Bathsheba, was suitable in God's eyes. I think the point of this lesson from scripture is that God gets to choose who will build His habitation along with all the details of it. Solomon's life was not perfect. He didn't have the honour of being called a man after God's own heart, but he was a man of peace. God gave him the desire of his heart, as he humbly asked to lead the people of God with wisdom. The attitude of humble dependence on God, peace with those around you, and being chosen for a task, are elements that God desires of those who would make a habitation for Him.

The amazing thing to me is that we actually do house God the Spirit, not in a temporary way, which is dependent on our deeds and obedience. We are the permanent vessel for God's Spirit. I wonder how "at home" God is in our midst? Our focus and worship make us more aware of His presence for sure, but I wonder if we sometimes grieve the Spirit, who is love and grace. He embodies all the fruit of the Spirit and so much more. When we act in pride, or negativity is He less comfortable among us?

Though striving to improve may be a human response to those questions, it will not create the environment God chooses as His home. We can only please and serve His desires by listening to Him and adjusting our hearts to His. Listening, yielding to Him and honouring His presence, invites Him to furnish us with the furniture of Heaven: Heavenly love, joy, peace, righteousness and such, are the comforts for His pleasure. This open attitude of invitation to His penetrating presence in every area of our soul, will establish us, individually and together, as God's place of rest.

Listening Prayer/Meditation Exercise (Personal Connection)

How is my level of righteousness, peace and joy in each of the following areas?

My God connection?

My relationships?

Finances?

Work, business or ministry?

Listening Prayer/Meditation Exercise (Corporate Connection)

How at home is God in our midst? Do we sense His pleasure in our meetings?

Do we see corporate answers to prayer?

Is there growth among us spiritually /numerically?

Do we sense our corporate calling to the community around us?

Is Holy Spirit free to flow through every believer present?

9 – Identity

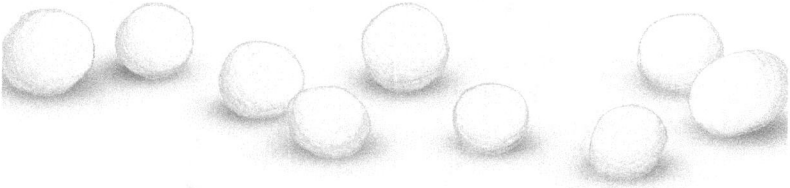

Real Life

God expresses His generous nature through His creation. His life is imparted and imputed into what He creates. As human beings we are created with His blue print, made in His image, so we actually reflect back to Him His own nature. We are created by love to reflect love. Our actual nature and design is built for love. God has designed us to default to kindness, mercy, joy, peace, purity and most basic love and trust. Love is our souls perfect fuel. We can see why it is so painful to be separated from this state of perfect love and how our world is disjointed and groaning in trivial for the restoration of its design.

If come to the topic of personal identity through the lens of examining ourselves we begin through a broken view of self. Let's instead gaze through the perfect lens of God's original design, before the fall of mankind and the separation between perfect love and our souls. God's original design was union between God and human kind. He created us for fellowship, unified in spirit with Him, in agreement with His way of living and at peace with Him and our surroundings.

What an amazing life Adam and Eve first had in the beauty of pristine creation unbroken communion with the Father and every need met perfectly. This life in union with God is available now. It is God's desire and design

Autonomous Self (Self I)

- Separate
- Needs to control
- Lives in lack, need, pain and sin
- Needs to be satisfied
- Grasps for people and things
- Makes decisions based on facts, feelings and fear of the options of others
- Self righteous
- Needs more external approval, accumulation of wealth, possessions or accolades for happiness
- Self must be righteous by effort and striving. Religious rules and rituals are believed to prove righteous by obedience to laws and duty

True Self (One with God/Christ I)

- Unified in God
- God controls, I yield
- Lives in peace and abundance
- Is satisfied at one's core
- Goes to God for approval
- Lives from the voice and unction of God, obeys God's directives, does not need others to approve
- Lives in Christ's righteousness
- Less is OK, being diminished makes no difference, happiness comes from living in Christ
- Only God is righteous, lives without guilt covered in Christ
- We are already loved and approved of by God. Religion does not make us more worthy, obedience is an act of love

even though the earth is not in its former unpolluted state our souls capacity is restored by the reconciliation work of Jesus Christ. We can be unified with God and can live today as one with Him.

As we look to His original design, we are actually looking into His nature alive in us. God has created us in His image, therefore we are like Him especially as we choose to live in union (agreement) with His nature in us.

On the above pages you will note a comparison chart of what a person may picture or think their relationship is to God. You will note the autonomous self (Self I) views themselves as separate from God which is the case before we have been reconciled to God through faith in Jesus Christ. The next illustration is of the true self (Christ I) which depicts the true position of those who have given their lives to Christ. We are not longer separated due to the presence of the indwelling Spirit of God. Our nature is changed so that we may enjoy the benefits of unbroken fellowship with God.

Our true nature (as people who are born of the Spirit of God) is the unified self. If we view ourselves as the autonomous self (see figure on the next page) we think and act separately from God. We are living from human carnal nature (ego centric). Believing we are separate therefore not tapping into the nature of God, will cause us to hugely underachieve. God has designed us to live in union with Him so that together we live above the limits of human reasoning and abilities. The truth of us being one with God will shift us into His divine nature so that we look to Holy Spirit to live through us instead of living from our human nature alone. Most of us dance between these two views of self and that's okay as long as we keep progressing into spiritual reality. Forgetting who we really are is common but it does lose ground until we recover true vision.

"Don't let anyone lead you astray with empty

philosophy and high-sounding nonsense that come from human thinking and from the evil powers of this world, not from Christ. For in Christ the fullness of God lives in human body, and you are complete through your union with Christ." Colossians 2:8–10

Shifting our focus from self toward God is not a naturally easy process. It actually goes against our human nature to turn from self. The difficulty comes from many areas and is humanly quite hard, if not impossible, to surmount. However, our Maker has made the way through the renewal that comes by way of new birth by the Spirit of Jesus Christ. When His Holy Spirit joins with ours (by our permission) God infuses our soul to help us turn from self-focus (self I) to God focus (Christ I). We become new creatures, no longer alone. The "self I" becomes the "Christ I" in truth. However, we must come into that knowledge and understanding then we will notice this new nature within us.

Our minds need to shift to access His presence. We need to be present to access Presence. Being present in the moment is the only way to connect with God who is the I Am. God is available now. In the same moment you are in at this moment He is, which is the difficulty we have. So often we are fixated on the past or looking into what may be in the future therefore we miss the present moment.

This dilemma of being present to access the Presence is one our spiritual mothers and fathers have always faced. The ancients developed methods and practices to help them connect moment by moment to the Eternal Present One. As we continue my prayer is that we will learn to practice some tried and true methods as well as experiment with some more recent practices. The point of these exercises is that each person may find the best helps for them currently and will develop particular ways of being present so as to connect with God. As we allow

God to mould our hearts by His presence we bring joy our great King Jesus. After all it was for the joy set before Him that Jesus endured the agony of separation – that we may be *one*.

Listening Prayer/Meditation Exercise
Father God please speak to me about my true identity.

10 – Fruit

There are around 200 Scripture references to fruit. In the Old Testament and the New these references refer to natural fruit (which grows from plants), the fruit of a person's life (the results of how they have lived) and spiritual fruit (both good and bad). The fruit or results of living a connected life have an interesting correlation to the trees in the Garden of Eden.

> *The Lord God made all kinds of trees grow out of the ground—trees that were pleasing to the eye and good for food. In the middle of the garden were the tree of life and the tree of the knowledge of good and evil. Genesis 2:9*

We all know the story of Adam and Eve; that they ate the fruit of the forbidden tree. Knowledge of good and evil was its name and that fruit imparted to them its namesake. Before that the tree of Life and all the other fruit of the garden had been satisfying. Now their understanding had expanded to things that brought fear of punishment, shame, and enmity – not the "enlightenment" the tempter promised. The fruit of the knowledge of good and evil bore bad results just as God warned them. Partaking of that fruit had spiritual, physical and emotional ramifications.

Here we are today in the 21st century, still affected and infected with this fruit, the knowledge of good and evil, which causes us to judge everything and everyone. We weigh up with our human logic and knowledge the worth of others and ourselves. We consider actions and think we can evaluate motivations to satisfy our need to understand, but instead we bear the fruit of that judgment ourselves.

> *Jesus said: "Do not judge, or you too will be judged. For in the same way you judge others, you will be judged, and with the measure you use, it will be measured to you."*
> *Matthew 7:1–2*

That fruit, eaten by our original ancestors, has a very nasty after taste that lingers. It is similar to the generational sin issue Israel had.

> *"What do you people mean by quoting this proverb about the land of Israel: "The parents eat sour grapes, and the children's teeth are set on edge?" Ezekiel 18:2*

God corrected the thinking of that day; that the children of sinners get punished for their parents' sins. However, it's worth noting that the residue of sin did not lift from the children, due to the fact they were born into sin through the fall and would therefore sin because of it. God was just letting them know He would judge according to each person's merit. Without the substitutionary death of Jesus Christ, we would all still be under God's judgment. Now we are forgiven and have freedom to live reinstated into the garden. Once again free to choose which tree we will partake of.

Jesus divine flow (Holy Spirit) is the tree of life. Human thinking is the tree of the knowledge of good and evil. We who are born of God may now choose to live from the tree of life by partaking of His nature and listening to His direction. When we tap into the tree of life we bear the fruit of that tree; spiritual, physical and emotional life.

This life manifests in our souls as Christlikeness.

Picking the Best Fruit

Perhaps you are wondering how to pick the right fruit to eat? How about we ask another question? How did we pick the wrong fruit to begin with? Answer: By choosing human reasoning rather than what God said, mankind chose wrongly. When we pick human judgment and reasoning instead of what God says about something we are picking the wrong fruit to eat. In order to choose well we need to turn our focus back to what God says. In the beginning mankind had freedom to choose because they had not been tainted by the rebellion of ignoring God's words. However, when tempted Eve noticed the fruit was good to look at and she reasoned it would be a better choice so she picked it and they ate it. We have been welcomed back into the garden and again been given complete freedom to eat from any tree, except the tree of our own understanding (knowledge of what we deem as good and evil). That tree brings the bad fruit of judgment on us. Choosing to heed God's words and partake of the life Christ gives us delivers the sweet fruit of the Spirit. When we listen to God and live according to His design we pick the fruit from the tree of life. Then our lives flourish in every way. We begin to bear evidence of the divine life we have partaken of by inviting Holy Spirit to live in us. Holy Spirit is the bearer of supernatural fruit, which begins to sprout within, producing the life of Christ. Jesus is, as we know, the Life.

Divine life is our portion. It is God's intention that we eat of His life every day and that we live in communion as Adam and Eve did before the fall. In fact, we can now have even greater access to this life, due to the fact that we are already partakers of it, through Holy Spirit's indwelling. The choice is there is no separation for we have returned to the Garden of God. Jesus has opened the way for us to have unbroken friendship with our Heavenly Father but we must choose to eat well. We will bear the fruit of our daily choices whether it be the abundant life of the Spirit in agreement with God or the limitation of human understanding leading to judgment. When we focus on the best tree we will harvest divine life.

Supernatural Fruit

As everyone knows if you plant or sow a particular type of seed in the ground it will produce in kind. For example; radish seeds produce radishes. The quality of the fruit and how much is produced is due to natural elements like; rain, temperature, sunlight and soil quality. If all these factors are suitable you will have an abundant yield of radishes. Natural seed produces the type of fruit or vegetable you have sown and yield is dependent upon varying environmental conditions.

Spiritual fruit grows in a similar way: In the case of spiritual gardening the soil is your soul (mind, will, emotions, conscience, and imagination). The seed is God's word, His essence and nature planted in you through the Holy Spirit. This supernatural seed of the Spirit produces a supernatural crop. Interestingly the amount of supernatural fruit we produce is not dependent upon the elements around as it is with natural seed (rain and sunlight etc.). It does not depend on our soil quality, for example, if our lives are in perfect order, if our environment is peaceful and conflict free, or even if we are hard working. The crop quality and abundance is due to our willingness to yield. We produce a good crop of spiritual fruit if we will yield to the work the Holy Spirit wants to do in us.

We cannot produce supernatural spiritual fruit from natural human seed. If we use love as our example: We desire to love others. If we are to love with God's love we must fuel up or be seeded with the love of God first. We must have the supernatural love of God thriving in us through connecting with God's love in our own hearts. Then we can draw upon that love for others. Otherwise our love will be merely human, natural love, produced by our human effort. We will be loving with human love, which is nice but far inferior to supernatural love.

It takes spiritual seed to produce supernatural fruit. The fruit of the Spirit is produced by supernatural seed from God's nature not from the natural human nature. We do not expect an apple tree to grow from radish seeds and so we cannot expect to produce supernatural love from human sources.

To Yield Spiritual Fruit We Must Yield Our Spirit and Soul To God.

Fruit that Attracts

The Fruit of Holy Spirit is the character and nature of God worked out in us supernaturally by Him. The beauty of the nature of God in us becomes a magnet that draws people. The world has nothing in comparison to supernatural love, joy, peace, patience, gentleness, goodness, faith, humility or moderation. People long for the peace and joy we embody. They love to be near us because they notice it in and around us. So, we become magnets for the lost, wounded, and searching people all around us. They are drawn to Him living in us and expressing through us.

I had the experience of being touched physically by strangers in different situations. People would want to touch my hair or jewellery or feel the texture of my clothing. It was a bit uncomfortable for me and I asked the Lord: "What's with this touching thing God? You know I feel uncomfortable being touched by strangers!"

God's reply to me was simple; "They want Me Yvonne, they feel Me in you. I am drawing them. Let it be a signal to you these ones are being drawn".

Fruit that Repels Evil

Supernatural attributes are powerful. We see from the word of God that "the weapons of our warfare are not carnal, but mighty through God to the pulling down of strong-holds." Corinthians 10:4. These weapons we are given are not obtained or made in natural or carnal way. We cannot produce weapons that fight our supernatural foe Satan. The only way to fight evil is with the resources of Heaven.

If we consider our enemies tactics, his weapons that kill, steal and destroy us are things like; hatred, depression, rage, impatience, violence, lust, doubt, pride and addiction to name just a few. However, we see in a list of God's characteristics His fruit is the antidote for everything evil can use to harm us. His fruit is the antidote for the negative feelings that attack our soul. When we are filled with Holy Spirit, there is no room for strongholds of evil: Jesus our deliverer casts out our enemies. For example:

- God's love cancels out hatred in our hearts, it drives out fear that probably caused hate.

- The joy of the Lord strengthens us to rise up against things like depression. Joy is God's calm delight as well as happiness.

- The peace of God quells rage and guards our hearts and minds as well.

- God's patience in our hearts overrides Satan's striving and impatience.

- Supernatural gentleness stands firm against violence. A gentle answer turns away wrath.

- The goodness of God leads us to repentance and integrity deals with dishonesty and sin.

- The faith of God moves enemy mountains of doubt and unbelief.

- Meekness or humility keeps us close to the heart of God so pride has no place.

- Holy Spirit control keeps our desires, needs, and passions in moderation and balance.

Against such amazing weapons there is no evil equal. No law of God will limit the amounts of such beautiful characteristics to be displayed and released through our lives each day. We can be sure these divine characteristics are heavens answer to bring hells strategies to naught. We need these attributes of God today in our hearts as well as out in the world. We who have the Holy Spirit living in our spirit have all we need for life and godliness all we need to do is agree with God and yield.

Fruit of Devotion

Blessed is the man who does not walk in the counsel of the wicked or stand in the way of sinners or sit in the seat of mockers. But his delight is in the law of the Lord and on his law he meditates day and night. He is like a tree planted by streams of water which yields its fruit in season and whose leaf does not wither. Whatever he does prospers.
Psalms 1:1–3

The first three verses from the first psalm in the Bible is a song of the virtues of devotion. There is blessing to be enjoyed by those who delight in God and meditate on His word. This person does not dry up from lack of spiritual watering. They will yield fruit in each season of life and will not fade away but remain vital and vibrant even till old age.

The righteous will flourish like a palm tree,
they will grow like a cedar of Lebanon;
planted in the house of the Lord they will still
bear fruit in old age, they will stay fresh and
green, proclaiming, "The Lord is upright;
he is my Rock, and there is no wickedness in
him." Psalm 92:12–15

Palm trees have extremely deep taproots and can withstand the most virulent storms because of their flexibility. The Cedar of Lebanon represents strength, endurance and spiritual depth. Only those who are truly righteous can be like this, but doesn't the scripture also say none are righteous not one? Righteousness is ours only because we are God's children adopted in through the covenant Jesus made by His blood.

Fruitful or Fitful

So, everyone who is under the new covenant through Jesus Christ is made righteous. But not every one of those has found delight in God as these saints have. Not every one who has Christ's righteousness imputed to them is flourishing in old age. Why is that? Not all choose to focus on Him. Unfortunately, many Christians are meditating more on themselves and the occupations of the world than on the Rock who is upright and Holy. Could it be that it is just easier to remain in the old human nature rather than turning to Jesus daily and building a life in devotion to Him? Often when we are fitful in our times with God (on one day and off the next) faith wanes and our hearts grow cold toward godly pursuits like reading meditating and communing with the Living Word (Jesus) Instead of the flame of passion being fanned it merely flickers. We become cold, so even though our spirit cries out like a baby needing to be fed, we turn away plugging our ears to its cry. Ignoring our spirits cry of hunger will eventually cause it to slump into fitful spiritual slumber. Some feed on religious pablum but religion is just filler with little spiritual substance. Religion feeds human nature and will not produce Godly fruit. Rousing the sleeping sonship inside only happens when real spiritual nourishment from El Shaddai the Breasted One. God alone is the strength giver. The true lover of our souls who can nurture us into fruit bearing.

Some of Jesus Words about Fruit:

"Produce fruit in keeping with repentance."
Matthew 3:8

Think of what you had to repent from when you first invited Christ to come into your life. He is saying to display that you have turned away from those behaviours. In other words, move on into maturity. If you are stuck you can ask Him to show you how to move forward.

"By their fruit you will recognize them. Do people pick grapes from thorn bushes, or figs from thistles? Likewise, every good tree bears good fruit, but a bad tree bears bad fruit. A good tree cannot bear bad fruit, and a bad tree cannot bear good fruit. Every tree that does not bear good fruit is cut down and thrown into the fire. Thus, by their fruit you will recognize them." Matthew 7:16–20

We can't produce fruit from the tree of life if we keep going to the tree of the knowledge of good and evil. The fruit of life is righteousness, peace and joy in the Holy Spirit. The fruit of human knowledge is judgment. We take our pick.

"Therefore, I tell you that the kingdom of God will be taken away from you and given to a people who will produce its fruit"
Matthew 21:43

Religion does not please God. It robs Him of true

devotion. Godly fruit produces kingdom results.

> *"Remain in me, as I also remain in you.*
> *No branch can bear fruit by itself; it must*
> *remain in the vine. Neither can you bear*
> *fruit unless you remain in me. I am the vine;*
> *you are the branches. If you remain in me*
> *and I in you, you will bear much fruit; apart*
> *from me you can do nothing." John 15:4–5*

Remaining in the Vine (Jesus Christ) is achieved by living in complete harmony with Him. We can live from Him as He lives in us through continual turning and tuning into His presence. Enjoying the abiding friendship and companionship of Holy Spirit is one of the many treasures of the Christian experience.

> *"This is to my Father's glory, that you bear*
> *much fruit, showing yourselves to be my*
> *disciples." John 15:8*

Bearing God's likeness (His Fruit) is the evidence that we are His disciples.

> *You did not choose me, but I chose you and*
> *appointed you so that you might go and*
> *bear fruit – fruit that will last – and so that*
> *whatever you ask in my name the Father will*
> *give you." John 15:16*

There are definitely advantages to this shared life in Christ. As we devote time, attention, energy and put our hope in God He strengthens us to rise above our difficulties and carries us into our destiny by His grace and power (Ps 29:11). We are chosen to be kingdom fruit bearers. We are chosen for favour and called to display Christ to the world through the fruit of our lives.

Listening Prayer/Meditation Exercise
Holy Spirit please speak to me about bearing Your fruit.

11 – Adversity

Living in Truth

There are some essential realities about God, and our identity, we need to remember as we journey through life. Foundational beliefs surface to enable us to walk triumphantly through the tough times of life. The lack of foundational truth brings disaster and extra emotional struggle in times of adversity. In fact, the lack of truth can be our downfall when trials come.

> *"Therefore, everyone who hears these words of mine and puts them into practice is like a wise man who built his house on the rock. The rain came down, the streams rose, and the winds blew and beat against that house; yet it did not fall, because it had its foundation on the rock. But everyone who hears these words of mine and does not put them into practice is like a foolish man who built his house on sand. The rain came down, the streams rose, and the winds blew and beat against that house, and it fell with a great crash." Matthew 7:24–27*

Some foundational truths about God, the believer and circumstances have been expounded in the previous chapters. All of these things serve to steady us throughout life – especially when we are going through hardship and times of instability. When things are shaking, only what is true remains. Eternal, unwavering truth has supernatural power to sustain us. Facts, like these listed below, are the rock on which our lives can be built.

- God is love and is loving. He loves me. God is in sovereign control of everything. God is kind and good and He is working everything together for my ultimate good.

- I am in partnership with Jesus Christ and He lives with me. I am connected and can commune with Him all the time. He is not a silent partner. He is sufficient and I am not.

- Holy Spirit is permanently united with my spirit. I can draw on the power of God from within me. I do not have to flounder in human resources. I can release supernatural resources and live like Jesus did on earth.

How to Live in the Substance of Things Not Presently Manifested

One of the first things we find naturally happening, when we hit adversity in life, is that we forget the realities just listed. We need to review these truths to remind ourselves of Who we belong to. Forgetting who we are often happens during times of adversity. Often we forget the power of God, and the partnership with Jesus Christ we are connected to. Our human inadequacies tend to dominate our thinking. We can be overwhelmed by circumstances and forget what is actually true.

Remember, I belong to God and He belongs to me

I belong to Him, and just as importantly, God (Father Son and Holy Spirit) belongs to me. I am family to Jesus Christ and as such I always have a place here on earth as well as in Heaven. I may be temporarily displaced from my place on earth, but the truth is I do belong and God has not disowned me, even if I feel that way. I am actually already seated in God, so I need to see myself that way all the time. It is an excellent practice to picture yourself in the Father, especially in times of adversity or displacement. The picture of you seated in Him is reality – more real than the temporary things you see here in this time frame.

Ask God what He says about your situation before you decide what you think about it

We often make wrong assumptions and judgments based on what we perceive is true. Sometimes the circumstances are horrendous. When we are in trauma, we are unable to work through the circumstantial reality and find true reality. In those times we especially need to hear what God says is true. This is where a daily practice of listening to God is a huge advantage because we already know what He sounds like. If we are used to His voice, we become accustomed to asking Him what His take is on a given situation. If we often ask God what He says is true, we will, even in trauma and grief, have an inkling of His kind heart for us. We will be able to grasp His perspective.

As we go through the journey of recovery from trauma or grief, God will position His family around us. Sometimes it comes as angelic help, but often He sends His friends to prophesy life and hope. If we receive these prophetic words, they will be a lifeline we can grab hold of to pull us up into the reality of life and hope.

When God speaks we must agree with His words, over and above our feelings and what the circumstances look like. This is the kind of faith that will move the mountains of doubt, unbelief, discouragement and undue grief.

To clarify, there is grief that is healthy and needs to be expressed, we are not talking about healthy grief here.

The role of prophesying over ourselves

Once we have discerned what God is saying about our circumstances, we must speak His words over them. I have, on many occasions, witnessed the shift in circumstances when the word of the Lord was prophesied over seemingly impossible situations. It seems heaven and earth are waiting for the sons of God to take the word of God seriously, decreeing in faith what God says is to happen.

Ezekiel 37 (Dry Bones Prophecy) is just one demonstration from Scripture of God requiring us to agree and speak His word into situations and lives. In fact, in Ezekiel 36:37 God tells Israel to ask Him for that which He is telling them they can have. This is important to note, because it is their act of faith in the word to ask God to do it. God is not saying:

> *"Now go make it happen you guys! Do what I've said will happen!"*

No, God is looking for faith in *His power* to act. He is waiting. He will not do what He said He would do, until we ask Him for it. At times I have not had enough faith to do that, but I've asked Him to help my unbelief. He answered that prayer for increased faith first, then stepped in and did what He wanted to do to as I agreed for it.

Abram did it every time he told people his new name – because His new name meant the father of many nations. He surely was not that (at that moment). In earthly reality, at that time, he was the father of none. Eternity sees it all. All Abram's descendants were a reality in Heaven. What God says, is a reality already in Heaven, therefore we need to agree and speak it into earth.

There have been people who, though they thought it was scriptural to do so, have taught it is right to make demands that God fulfill what they feel are His obligations to man. God is so kind, patient and good. He really is not obligated to us at all. He has met all obligations-even those we are responsible for – through the sacrificial gift of eternal life Jesus fulfilled. We need to remember that He, if any, has the right to demand everything from us, yet He does not. It is our part to agree with what He says is true about the circumstances, then to speak over them and trust Him to work things together for His good purposes. God is not in debt to us. He holds all the trump cards and is giving them to us. Together we win!

Giving Thanks and Being a Blessing

Gratitude is a tool in the hand of God, to switch our focus from our insufficiency and difficulties, to His great abilities. When we find something good in hard times, and thank God, we change our negative, hopeless thoughts and open our eyes of faith to see His hand already working. There is always something He is doing for our good.

> *And we know that in all things God works*
> *for the good of those who love him, who*
> *have been called according to his purpose.*
> *Romans 8:28*

As we switch from negativity to God activity, we begin to be involved in life around us in a new way. We are not just surviving a trial we begin to thrive through it. I have noticed when people in hopeless situations begin to be grateful to God, even for just glimmers and glimpses of His work, they are opened up to see other people's needs. When I have asked hurting people to minister, even in the midst of their trial, they have found purpose again. They begin to rise up into sonship and rule over the circumstances.

Jesus modeled this so beautifully. He lived under the threat of death and persecution. *NO! He lived over it!* Just like Jesus, who's Spirit indwells us, we can live over and above adversity. This is very much a mind issue. If we will just shift from self-focus to God focus, we will be ready to be a blessing to others. This shift will bring us into overcoming grace. The biggest issue for us to overcome is self-focus.

Adversity Is Not What It Seems

Perspective comes in hindsight. God is with us. True, but He is also ahead in time, looking back on what you are going through. He is seeing what it looks like from eternity, therefore we need to get the facts straight. No one knows like God knows. Jacob (James the brother of Jesus) had insight and gave great advice.

> *Consider it pure joy, my brothers and sisters, whenever you face trials of many kinds, because you know that the testing of your faith produces perseverance. Let perseverance finish its work so that you may be mature and complete, not lacking anything. If any of you lacks wisdom, you should ask God, who gives generously to all without finding fault, and it will be given to you. But when you ask, you must believe and not doubt, because the one who doubts is like a wave of the sea, blown and tossed by the wind. That person should not expect to receive anything from the Lord. Such a person is double-minded and unstable in all they do.*

> *Believers in humble circumstances ought to take pride in their high position. But the rich should take pride in their humiliation— since they will pass away like a wild flower.*

For the sun rises with scorching heat and withers the plant; its blossom falls and its beauty is destroyed. In the same way, the rich will fade away even while they go about their business.

Blessed is the one who perseveres under trial because, having stood the test, that person will receive the crown of life that the Lord has promised to those who love him.

When tempted, no one should say, "God is tempting me." For God cannot be tempted by evil, nor does he tempt anyone; but each person is tempted when they are dragged away by their own evil desire and enticed. Then, after desire has conceived, it gives birth to sin; and sin, when it is full-grown, gives birth to death.

Don't be deceived, my dear brothers and sisters. Every good and perfect gift is from above, coming down from the Father of the heavenly lights, who does not change like shifting shadows. He chose to give us birth through the word of truth, that we might be a kind of first fruits of all he created. James 1:2–18

Listening Prayer/Meditation Exercise

What do You want to tell me about the times of adversity I have faced God?

Book 3: The Way

Snail Trail

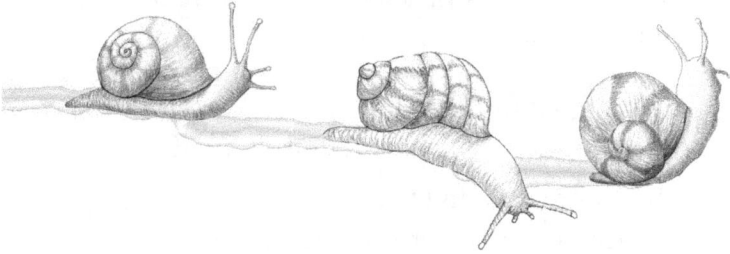

The way of life lived in union with Jesus Christ, is illustrated in this third book by the symbol of the humble garden snail. As a child, snails in my parent's garden fascinated me. I would most often see them on the garden path, in the damp of the morning dew. They would appear slowly, making their silent journey, on the gilded path their tiny, slug-like bodies created. I loved the way their eyes would move all around independently from one another. They were not bothered by inquisitive touches. They had their place of retreat always along for the ride. I would have so liked that then, a place of retreat, where I could hide when danger lurked.

Now I realize I have this beautiful life, like my little snail-friends have. I have my own garden path to glide upon, a place of beauty to retreat to always along with me. I am safe, and now have sight to see from many more angles than is humanly possible. God has put spiritual eyes in my heart that are opened to see what He shows me.

There is a sweet communion given as one slows the pace in life and comes in silence, solitude and gratitude. I realize now that many other dear little (human) snails have gone before – quietly, humbly, gliding along on the silvery trail of practice and discipline, so well-oiled by God. Please come follow them with me on their silver trail, if you will. The practices and disciplines of God's humble little loved ones will help us also, to find ways to stay focused on the Divine Lover. They are the trailblazers who searched for God's private garden, and have found it inside their own hearts.

Silvery Trailblazer
Drawn by the morning mist to find,
My silently moving friend.
Looking to see where she might be,
There is the glimmering blend
Down on the garden path she slides,
Her silvery footprint sends
A message to me,
Come let me see,
This path so attractively bends.
I crouch down to watch her so gracefully carry,
Her safe place,
I'm tempted to touch,
She is such a story, so free from all worry,
I ponder the way she has been.
For I too must go the pathway unknown,
Perhaps she will share of her story,
And I'll learn her way to gracefully stay,
In moments, in step with God's glory.

Spiritual Disciplines and Practices

Spiritual practices and disciplines are actions or activities regularly used to move us along the path of spiritual growth. Some of these include; listening prayer, meditation, fasting, and extended times with God, such as retreat and pilgrimage. Many practices incorporate silence, solitude, singing and gratitude. All are considered spiritual disciplines that strengthen, deepen and give vitality to faith.

Without spiritual practices, we find ourselves struggling against the current of modern life to find intimacy with God. If we look back into history, we will note practices, which earnest seekers of God used to connect with His presence. Focused attention on God is needed now more than ever, but practice and discipline are missing from many of our lives. Probably the biggest factor in this missing element is that these tools have not been passed on. Some of these methods are laid out in this section called "The Way".

New practices have, through time, been introduced. As you journey on this path you may also discover new ways to commune intimately with God. Whether we use the tried and tested methods of the past, or experiment with new practices, the thing to remember is: *the focus of practices or disciplines is connecting with the presence of God*, (Father, Son and Holy Spirit). *Methods are just the means to settle into Him.* If the discipline of practicing a method perfectly becomes the focus, we have missed the main point of spiritual practices. Today many people are "Gurus" of contemplation, meditation and stillness, but sadly they are void of intimacy with God. Even Bible study can become just an exercise in pulling apart the scriptures. Theoretically learning about God misses the goal of experiencing the living God, who wants to speak truth and renew our minds. Remember Jesus Christ is the living word and He is present and ready to speak to us now.

Spiritual practices help us remember who we are in Christ – that He is in us and present with us in each moment. These ways of connecting with God are not for us to grasp for something from Him, but more are ways of allowing God to have greater access to us. They give more room or create space (internally and in life) for Him.

1 – Silence

Drinking is the process of taking in, using the mouth, but in speaking we use the mouth in a very different way. One motion is the opposite to the other. Is it possible to drink through a straw and speak at the same time? Think about it. Our speech would not be very articulate and I'm sure not without a whole lot of mess. I think listening prayer, compared to our prayers to God, are also quite different processes. It is quite difficult to hear the still small voice (spontaneous thoughts) of God, if we are incessantly formulating prayers to Him. Even thinking words of worship may interfere with receiving His thoughts. Speaking or thinking our communications, prevents us from listening and really hearing His.

When we think of human conversations, people who listen to one another, giving each other proper attention, will have a better understanding of each other's points of view than those who interrupt or speak over each other. When conversations get heated, or emotions rise, listening may be happening, but hearing can be distorted. In such a case, our minds are often reloading thoughts to fire back as soon as our opponent takes a breath. Negative emotions rob us of the stillness and peace that is most conducive to hearing God. God can override our unrest to calm us, and often does. However, worry, anxiety, anger and other strong emotions tend to block us and cause confusion, which hampers our ability to correctly hear and discern what God is saying.

Taking these things into account, we can understand why much of our times trying to hear God are unsuccessful. The simple fact that we are not quiet in mind, or that we are emotionally stirred up creates too much internal noise. God can yell, but He mostly just waits patiently. Then, at last in moments of alertness to His presence, we capture His thoughts. If we are not aware of the problem, we may think God is silent most of the time. The truth is, God loves to communicate and is very articulate. It is our listening skill that is lacking. It is up to us to position ourselves to hear. As the following Scripture encourages us, we must pay attention to how we hear.

> *"So, pay attention to how you hear. To those who listen to my teaching, more understanding will be given. But for those who are not listening even what they think they understand will be taken away from them." Luke 8:18*

Jesus was teaching the crowd that had gathered. They could hear the sound of his voice but it was going over their heads. He drew attention to the fact that they were not really listening. Was it their inattention because they were distracted by the size of crowd or natural things? Was it their own internal issues that caused them to be critical of Him, or questioned his authority to teach? It may have been the simple fact they doubted He was from God. Whatever the issue was, it would have grave consequences for them. It caused them not to hear words that would give eternal life. Their inability to receive the words was due to how they heard. Their hearing was affected by their attentiveness and their receptiveness.

Silence is more than us not talking. It goes deeper, in respect of authority of the messenger and message, just as hearing is more than a brain function. Hearing at a heart level has spiritual effect that moulds our thinking and influences our way of life. When we wait in silence for God to speak, we give respect that creates a place for His presence. Not only do we hear or sense, we know God has met with us and we are changed. When a King speaks, no one interrupts. Perhaps, in the familiarity of our Father's good graces, we forget to reverence His presence and so miss the wonder of being with our dear King.

> *This is what the Sovereign Lord, the Holy One of Israel, says: "In repentance and rest is your salvation, in quietness and trust is your strength, but you would have none of it" Isaiah 30:15*

When we stop trying to fill the silence with thought or words, we position ourselves to receive from our king. Silence makes space. Silence allows the still small voice of God to penetrate and resonate in the crevasses of our soul. In silence we learn to trust and find rest.

Silence Exercise
Please speak to me Lord as I sit silently in your presence. Use whatever means through my senses to commune with me.

2 – Solitude

One day as Jesus was alone praying Luke 9:18

All through the Gospel accounts Jesus is inundated with crowds of people, clambering for various reasons: Many came from desperation, many came from curiosity, many came greedy for miracles and many came to Him as their only hope. Jesus was rarely alone once His ministry began, but when He could, we see him carving out time to be alone.

Jesus models solitude as a way to fulfill his desire for undivided focus on His Father in Heaven. He needed to hear and see what His Father was saying and doing, so attentive focus had to have been His passionate desire. With so much to accomplish and so much pressure from every side, He managed to escape for precious alone time.

Very early in the morning, while it was still dark, Jesus got up, left the house and went off to a solitary place, where he prayed. Simon and his companions went to look for him, and when they found him, they exclaimed: "Everyone is looking for you!"

Jesus replied, "Let us go somewhere else – to the nearby villages – so I can preach there also. That is why I have come." So he traveled throughout Galilee, preaching in their

*synagogues and driving out demons. Mark
1:35–39*

Here we note, Jesus got up very early in the morning to go to a solitary place to pray. Remember He was a man with all the human needs for rest, food and need of comfort too, but His desire for solitude with the Father drove him to find a place alone.

Finding solitude in our contemporary lives can be a challenge too. We need to carve out time alone for God even more than Jesus did then. Our lives are invaded and crowded too, now electronically. For many seemingly good reasons, we allow the barrage of information and chatter. Business emails, phone calls, texts, as well as educational and social media all compound our problem; that of too little alone time with God. If Jesus Christ wanted and needed time alone we surely do too.

> *Immediately Jesus made the disciples get into the boat and go on ahead of him to the other side, while he dismissed the crowd. After he had dismissed them, he went up on a mountainside by himself to pray. Later that night, he was there alone, and the boat was already a considerable distance from land, buffeted by the waves because the wind was against it.*
>
> *Shortly before dawn Jesus went out to them, walking on the lake. Matthew 14:22–25*

We find after time alone with God, Jesus did amazing wonders. After forty days in the wilderness alone, He passed the tests of temptation, and then we are told;

> *Jesus returned to Galilee, filled with the Holy Spirit's power Luke 4:14*

Jesus' time of testing and fasting at the beginning of His ministry, gave Him such empowerment that He soon became well known through the surrounding area. He taught in synagogues and had praise and favour everywhere He went.

> *At daybreak, Jesus went out to a solitary place. The people were looking for him and when they came to where he was, they tried to keep him from leaving them. But he said, "I must proclaim the good news of the kingdom of God to the other towns also, because that is why I was sent." And he kept on preaching in the synagogues of Judea.*
> *Luke 4:42–44*

Jesus purpose was focused and firmly implanted, because He took time in solitude to align with His Fathers plan. He was a man passionately in possession of His purpose. Perhaps our generation of Christ followers can also benefit from times of solitude, to envision us and impart focus for purpose.

Solitude is a discipline that singles out and honours the One on whom we choose to spend our time. Being away from others to gather our own thoughts and have a rest is humanly quite helpful from time to time, but it is not why Jesus practiced it. There is a special humility found alone in the presence of God that causes us to get real like nothing else.

Choosing to be alone with God can be very difficult. We have to face the risk of loneliness, boredom, as well as our fears and insecurities. Like Jesus, we have a test to pass in our solitary wilderness. He chose it, and so must we. The reasons we need to have time alone to be with God have not changed for us in all the centuries since Jesus time. The Presence of God is our source of peace, power and love. When we take the initiative to be alone with Him we are showing a level of devotion that is very precious to God.

But when you pray, go into your room, close the door and pray to your father, who is unseen. Then you Father, sees what is done in secret, will reward you. Matthew 6:6

Alone in God's presence we drop the religious façade. When we have no human reward for our expressions of love, gratitude and worship to God it is truly authentic devotion. When an act of love is given to the Beloved, He views it as a precious and sacred gift.

Solitude Exercise
How can solitude help me God to connect with you better?

Show me Jesus how I can set apart time and space to follow your example of being alone with our Father.

3 – Gratitude

*Give thanks to the Lord, for he is good; his
love endures forever. 1 Chronicles 16:34*

Take just a moment. Stop reading and ponder what you
have right now to be thankful for. Think on the love God
has for you right now. He created you with love in His
heart and all His thoughts of you are good. Good is all
around you if you will ask God to show you.

Many times, life hands us extremely difficult
circumstances: sickness, financial stress, betrayal,
and even death, which can send us plummeting into
depression and hopelessness. But God has medicine that
will lift us up.

*Give thanks in all circumstances; for this
is God's will for you in Christ Jesus. 1
Thessalonians 5:18*

God's ways can be quite a mystery but His will is not. His
will is to bless you with joy unspeakable and full of glory
as the King James Bible says.

*Whom having not seen, ye love; in whom,
though now ye see him not, yet believing, ye
rejoice with joy unspeakable and full of glory
1 Peter 1:8 King James Version (KJV)*

If we read the beginning of that chapter we will see Peter
is writing to the believers in Asia and Bithynia who were

being persecuted and tested in "fiery trials". Peter was encouraging them. As they love and trust in God, He will bring them into supernatural glorious joy. It is the heart attitude of gratitude that turns our sorrows and trials into beauty.

Gratitude releases us from the entanglements of judgments. We can make wrong judgments about our circumstances, about those who cause us pain, about ourselves and even about God. When life is arduous and we are being tested, finding peace and rest in gratitude will rescue our hearts and keep us open to God.

I found this to be true when I experienced the pain and loss of miscarriage. I was in my late thirties when, over a two-year period, I lost several babies. We were blessed to be the parents of four beautiful children. We were Christians and trusted God, but we were not as mature as we needed to be and so God had a journey for us.

After the first miscarriage, I felt disallowed from grieving the loss. It seemed I should just get over this. After all it was so early on and I did have four beautiful healthy children. So, I pushed through and brushed off my emotions. Within a year we were blessed by the birth of our fifth child who brought so much joy that the loss seemed to disappear.

As time went on several more miscarriages occurred. These were much later in the pregnancies, and people knew. Even more difficult, our children knew. They were very disappointed. Each time we grieved as a family, with many tears and difficult attempts at explaining why. With each failed pregnancy, I had a birth to recover from and medical procedures to go through. I was not really well for those two years, struggling through lack of energy and repeated pregnancy symptoms like nausea. Each time I had to come to terms with the possibility of a new child, to overcome fear of death of that child and begin to accept and love the life inside me. With each death the grief and the loss mounted.

All Things Work Together For Good?

"There has to be something positive about this", the thought occurred as I lay on a gurney in the hall of our overcrowded local hospital. My latest baby had died and now I was in labour to deliver him. That thought, "There has be something positive about this," was a God thought. I could not have formulated it in the state of mind and body I was in at that moment. But, there it was, not even a question – a statement. It was answered by some words that I did not remember reading but instinctively knew were scripture.

> For I know the plans I have for you," declares
> the Lord, "plans to prosper you and not
> to harm you, plans to give you hope and a
> future. Jeremiah 29:11

That was my lifeline of hope. God would bring me through. I would not die (though I felt I might). I would go home to my family. I had such gratitude for the five beautiful children I had been given. I had such gratitude for a husband who loved me and was doing his best to support us. But I was not so sure about God.

I had tried to figure out why. What kind of God is this? He has allowed me to become pregnant knowing these babies would die, knowing the stress grief and illness that would follow. Was God mean? Did He love, or even like me? Were we being punished? What was I not understanding that I had to keep going through this lesson?

So many questions surfaced, but even with the questions, gratitude remained. That is what sustained my faith. Sweetness, even among the questions, pervaded my heart as I enjoyed the family I still had. A rich trust came that deepened my life like nothing else could have.

I did find out why. It was nothing like any answer I thought would come. It was good and I still sense God in it every time I mull it over. It was for the praise of His glory through me. My heart was taken through the fire of trial and has turned a sweeter colour of gold. I would not have connected with my lack of spiritual depth, I would not have learned how to hear His voice, and I could not have grown any other way than through that perfect fire.

Does God cause such grief and suffering? I don't believe so. However, He knows it's coming and He allows it for my good. I trust Him to keep refining my heart because He is good and His mercy endures forever. I have learned the power of gratitude.

Gratitude is a weapon and a healing balm that positions us to go deeply into God's heart.

Exercise in Gratitude
Ask God how you can express gratitude to Him, then take time to do it.

4 – Time

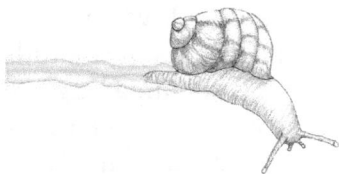

When I ponder expressing gratitude to God, I have wondered what I own that I can gift to Him. I wondered what He would want that I have to give. God really doesn't need or want my possessions or money. Although giving of my material wealth is an act of love and thanksgiving, it is not something God can use for His edification. The substance we have to give that He may enjoy is more personal: our time, which He has given to us to spend however we want. Time is limited and therefore is precious.

When I first thought about giving God my time, I pondered how long would be right for me to spend. In the Old Testament people were to give 10% of their income into the temple. An offering or love gift is not legislated by percentages, but I started to feel perhaps I could begin to give 10% of my day. Not as a tithe but as an offering of love. I began to give to God around 2 1/2 hours each day. It seemed at first to be such a difficult length of time to spend but, as I began to practice listening prayer, soaking, meditation, along with bible reading, walking, dancing in worship and fasting, the time seemed hardly enough. I began to experience God in such sweet and tangible ways. My motive was to give God pleasure. To my surprise, my time in His presence became an unexpected reward to me. In fact, the time was so precious to me I began to organize my life to accommodate not only hours each day, but a day alone with God each week.

One would think I couldn't possibly have accomplished much in life, since the devotion of much time and attention was given to God, but the opposite became true. When I began to give 10% of my day to God, I was home educating three of our five children. That in itself is a full-time commitment. I noticed something quite amazing. The more time I dedicated to God, the more I managed to accomplish in the remaining time. God stretched my time, much like He did my money when we gave a generous financial gift.

Heaven has an economy that is counter to logic. When we lavish our time, attention and other resources on God, He multiplies what remains. He loves to bless supernaturally, to show His pleasure. I encourage you to lavish your time and attention on the Father. He will draw you into the beauty of His affection – not that you are earning His love, but that His delight in those times of intimacy is tangible.

Giving Attention

Our attention is truly ours to give, as God has given us freedom to focus where we want to. We can choose to make His pleasure our priority. Amazingly, God really wants our attention and He loves it when we spend our time lavishly on Him. When we hurry through our devotional time and give scattered attention, the quality of our relationship with Him lacks depth. Jesus did not rush through His duty to us but gave it His all. He focused His attention and energy on all of us and sacrificed so much more than we can fathom. Jesus is still devoted to us. It seems such a small act of gratitude to give the things He longs to receive.

One of the issues that is common to us is that our attention wanders into other time zones. God is in this present moment in time, ready to commune with us now. The problem is that, even though He was with us in the past and will be with us when we get to the future, those are not our current experience. Present moment communion requires our minds to be present. God is present here and now; our minds must be with Him to experience His presence. Distraction, though we may enjoy old memories, will rob us of the time set aside (devoted) to God. Moments fly by and life must continue (unless of course we are on Retreat or some other extended spiritual sojourn). Attention is a gift we need discipline to give. God will give us grace to attain full attentiveness, as we give Him permission to work in our souls

Planning and pondering future events is necessary in life. I have to plan, sometimes years ahead, but if I ponder and picture future events too much I find, when the time does come and the event takes place, it is never as I had precisely envisioned it to be. I have been disappointed or at times, pleasantly shocked, at what God will actually do when the time comes. I can actually get in the way of His plans with my own dreams or vision of the event. Thankfully God does give revelation along the way to correct me however, I have learned too much planning is wasted time. God will do His work and I will watch in awe. So, I may as well mind my business in the present moment enjoying what we (He and I) are doing right now.

Something I've noticed along the way, a fringe benefit of giving full attention to God is I give attention to people more fully. Have you ever experienced a conversation with someone who is mentally not present with you? Even though they are looking at you, nodding as if they are listening, they are not hearing what you are saying. That is not much of a conversation at all. Sadly, I was guilty of being a pretending listener too. When we learn the discipline of attentiveness to the present moment it has the effect of enhancing all of our relationships, especially the supernatural one.

We are such a blessed people, to have a Father who loves to be with us, who enjoys us just because He loves us. It can be so delightful to linger in His presence, learning to give Him our full attention. Enjoying the life of being present in His delight is worth far more than the cost to us. Lavishing time and giving attention to His presence throughout our days will give us way more than it costs.

Dedication of Time Exercise

As you ponder your gift of time to God, you may ask Him what is best to offer. At times we can be legalistic, but God would rather a gift from the heart so allow Him to give you the amount that is best.

5 – Contemplation

Contemplation is a practice that takes dedicated time and focus. Contemplation connects with God through all of our senses, not only the mind, but our spirit soul and body are all involved. It differs from meditation in that meditation activates the mind. The mind is the receiver in meditation though the activity of inner sight, hearing and other senses. Contemplation is beholding God with all of ourselves. We receive revelation during contemplative practice holistically. We often need to interpret after, through talking it over with God in journaling or other listening practices.

The terms listening prayer, stillness, waiting on the Lord, and soaking in God's presence are terms for very similar practices within the realm of contemplative practice. These terms all involve the practice of extended stillness that brings the contemplative positioning of our soul. As was mentioned contemplation employs all of the senses without purposely centering the mind on a Scripture or pondering a particular line of thought.

Becoming still or being quiet inwardly, allows us to focus on God and hear Him. Soaking in God's presence is the current term for stillness for an extended period (usually one or two hours). Being still before God was practiced by the ancients, and has many references in Scripture:

> *Psalm 2:1–3 The Lord is my shepherd; I shall not want. He makes me to lie down in green*

pastures; He leads me beside the still waters. He restores my soul...

Psalm 27:14 Wait on the Lord; be of good courage and He shall strengthen your heart. Wait I say, on the Lord!

Psalm 37:7 Rest in the Lord and wait patiently for Him.

Psalm 131:2 Surely, I have calmed and quieted my soul, like a weaned child and his mother; like a weaned child is my soul within me.

Proverbs 1:33 But whoever listens to Me will dwell safely, and will be secure without fear of evil.

Isaiah 40:29 He gives power to the weak, and to those who have no might He increases strength. Even the youths shall faint and be weary, and the young men shall utterly fall, but those who wait on the Lord shall renew their strength. They shall mount up with wings like eagles. They shall run and not be weary; they shall walk and not faint.

Hosea 2:14 Therefore, behold, I will allure her. I will bring her into the wilderness and speak comfort to her.

Matthew 11:28–30 Come to Me, all you who labour and are heavy laden, and I will give you rest. Take My yoke upon you and learn from Me, for I am gentle and lowly in heart, and you will find rest for your souls. For My yoke is easy and my burden is light.

Luke 10:39 And she had a sister called Mary, who sat at Jesus' feet and heard His word.

> *Hebrews 4:9–11 There remains therefore*
> *a rest for the people of God. For who has*
> *entered His rest has himself also ceased*
> *from his works as God did from His. Let us*
> *therefore be diligent to enter that rest.*

We see soaking, or listening prayer with music in the presence of the Lord, modeled by Elisha the prophet.

> *"Now bring me someone who can play the*
> *harp." While the harp was being played, the*
> *power of the Lord came upon Elisha, and*
> *he said, "This is what the Lord says." Kings*
> *3:15–16*

David the Psalmist too knew the value and delight of resting in God's presence with an attitude of worship. In 1 Samuel 16:14–22, David "soaked" King Saul with music to bring him into peace and stillness. Like many of us, David was not a perfect person, yet he pleased God, who called him a man after His own heart.

Levels of Stillness

Becoming still is the process of quieting the inner being. To accomplish inner quiet, we often need to settle outer distractions and then to focus inwardly. We move our attention inward; from the outer body to quieting the soul (mind, will, emotions, imagination and conscience) so as to commune with the Holy Spirit Who indwells our human spirit.

In order for us to enjoy communion with God, to hear His voice through tuning inward to Holy Spirit, we need to hush the noise around us and within us. Following are some simple steps that may assist you as you learn to become still and hear God.

Allow time: As you learn to relax and meet with God, you will need to dedicate some time to the process.

Time constraint can cause unrest. Clock watching is a distraction that can be removed by setting a timer. Give yourself 10 to 15 minutes to settle into awareness.

Remove outer distractions: It is best, at first, to be alone, as electronic devices, phone calls, the movement of other people and pets will cause interruptions. Gather things you may need: pen, notepad, glass of water and perhaps a blanket for warmth.

Make yourself physically comfortable, since issues with body comfort can cause restlessness. For you, rest could be a position of lying down, sitting, standing or walking. While each body knows which position suits it best, choose one that is different from your normal sleep posture (if lying down is what's most comfortable). For those who feel most relaxed while walking, choose a quiet, solitary place to stroll.

Remove inner distractions: Relax; put a little smile on your lips. You may want to whisper the name of Jesus several times to focus your thoughts. Perhaps you will not need any further steps before you begin to sense God.

For some, however, this is when the mind begins to flit about, or go into activity. Don't try to force the quieting of the mind, just listen to the thoughts and see what the issue is. If you need to address distractions of the mind, ask Holy Spirit, "What are my thoughts?" Listen to the thoughts that flow from the question. He will reveal any area of concern.

Quietening Common Concerns

For worry: Give the concern over to God in prayer. Tell Him you trust Him to hold the issue (or person) for your time together. Picture the concern in God's hands and command worry to be silent in the name of Jesus.

For the to-do list: Simply write the list down and allow your mind the peace of knowing you will not forget but will get to the list later.

People for whom you may pray: Even the needs of others must be put on hold for the time being. Just make a note of the names and purpose to pray for them. This is your time to personally connect and hear God's heart for you.

Sin consciousness: Awareness of sin and our own inadequacies can be a barrier to meeting with God. God has provided very excellent help for us in that Jesus has more than paid for our debt with His sinless life poured out on the cross. Just bring yourself to Him afresh and agree with Him for your cleansing and restoration. Receive your forgiveness. Allow Him to wash over you in loving acceptance and move into communion with Him unhindered.

Remember that condemnation, guilt, and shame are not sent from God. He takes you as you are. By His precious blood, you are now fully accepted into His family as a son and heir. Your inheritance is now to fully enjoy your Father, and allow Him to fully enjoy communion with you.

Dedication Prayer: You may want to use the following prayer, or pray in your own words.

"Thank You for Your love and acceptance of me as Your child. I dedicate this time to be with You. Lord, I am listening. I am Yours and You are my God. The voice of a stranger and the voice of the enemy I will not hear. Thank You that I have the mind of Christ. I give You permission now, Holy Spirit, to supersede my thinking and speak to me through all of my faculties. I open myself up to You – Father, Son, and Holy Spirit. Amen."

Worship and Attune: Gratitude and worship (admiration for God and His ways) are the doorway into communion. Allow your mind to settle into thoughts of God, His attributes, His love and kindness toward you. Tell Him inwardly how you feel about Him. Whisper His name and inwardly welcome His presence. Tune in to flowing thoughts, pictures, and feelings. Relax and receive. You may now transition into soaking or listening prayer:

Contemplation Exercise

Enter into stillness. Ask God to speak to you about practicing beholding Him with your whole being.

Holy Spirit, speak to me about hearing You through an avenue I have not yet experienced.

6 – Meditation

Meditation is the ancient practice of exercising the mind in pondering a concept or Scripture. Christian meditation's goal is to slow down to connect with God. Meditation focuses our mind and spirit, bringing us to an attentive state so that we may digest truth and realign to God's perspective. As we offer God a dedicated, focused gift of time, the Holy Spirit brings us into alignment. He adjusts our inner stance toward God's way of thinking. The Spirit of God brings us into agreement with the mind of Christ, which is alive within every believer of Jesus Christ. Our minds and hearts need to adjust daily toward our greater purpose. The by-product of this reconnected relationship is inner peace.

Christian meditation is an active process of the soul (mind, will, emotions, imagination, and conscience). Unlike Eastern religious meditative practices, it is not emptying the mind of thought and overcoming physical distractions, but filling, refuelling, and communing with God our Creator. This inner process of meeting with and "hearing" God allows God's thoughts to reorder our thoughts. Through this process we may recognize where adjustments need to be made. Meditation gives the Spirit of God freedom to move truth and revelation to a deeper level within us, so that truth seeds and activates change within us. Our minds are renewed by the activation of truth enlightening, convincing, and convicting us.

Taking in the truths of God is more effective through

meditation because all of the faculties of the soul are involved. A focused but relaxed approach of meditation activates all of the soul's faculties: whereas the work and exercise of study involves the mind through human reasoning alone. Human reasoning is limited to what we know.

The process of Christian meditation, on Scripture for example, is similar to the activity of memorization with the added benefit of inviting the flow of Holy Spirit into the process. Not to merely get the words exact in the mind, then to use human reasoning to think about the meaning, but to include Holy Spirit's interjection, explanation, and expansion of our understanding. Meditation invites Him to interact with our senses, bringing the scripture or topic alive, through Spirit to spirit revelation internally teaching us. Our stilled and quieted soul is enabled to digest truth as we give God time and focused attention. In order to truly take in spiritual food, we must cease from our human striving and let our inner man feed, or drink in, the things God wants to teach us.

A helpful picture of this process is to view the difference between our normal process of thinking and learning with the contrasting picture of the meditative process of pondering truth. For example, when we use our reasoning abilities to think through a scripture we begin at point A, which examines the whole passage or verse. Then, through a process of study (perhaps researching with a concordance or Greek/ Hebrew dictionary), we break down the information within the passage and decide what it is telling us. Point B may be some insight that will cause us to research other things. Point C will lead us to D, E and so on, till we reach our conclusion at Z. This way of examining the scripture, studying it, is rather like a straight line (Linear thinking) as below.

A • B • C ••• Z

The meditative process is quite different. We begin at the same point (A), examining the passage or verse, but instead of only using the reasoned approach, studying and researching, we apply what I call circular thinking. Meditation employs the brain, but does not *work* at reasoning as with studying. The brain is occupied by repeatedly lifting scripture into the consciousness and receiving the thoughts and impressions from Holy Spirit. The Spirit of God overlays the fragments of scripture with deepening meaning, allowing the brain and soul to process each nugget of revelation and internalize them. As we begin reading or replaying the passage several times-- in its entirety at first, then following the Spirit, the brain gradually narrows down our focus to fewer and fewer words or fragments of scripture. A picture of this process would look like a spiral.

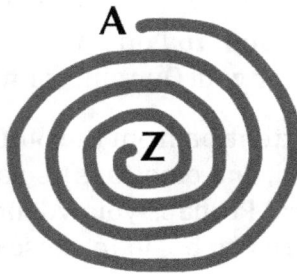

Point A > Z is at the center. We begin at the outer edge, but as we progress deeper into the center of the spiral, the rotation becomes shorter. The shorter length, or the spiral, represents fewer words repeated. In the simplicity of less, comes the beauty of the Holy revelation ever deepening in the soul and spirit. A little like the way a cow chews her cud, regurgitating it over and over to digest it fully, so is this process. The meditative process of spiritual digestion is that truth becomes part of our inner-man.

As with study, the meditative process can take us several sessions to unwrap a passage, depending upon how long a passage we are choosing to ponder. It is best to start with just one thought or verse at a time. If we do choose larger passages be prepared to take several sessions to complete the meditation.

Simple Steps for Biblical Meditation

Become still: quieting yourself is a process of first removing, as much as possible, any outer distractions such as:

Time constraints: set a time to avoid clock watching. Prepare people who may need your attention as to how long you need solitude, so they will be at peace.

Telephone and electronic devices need to be off.

Be physically comfortable, so pain or discomfort does not demand your attention. You do not have to be physically still if it is painful for you. Our aim is inward stillness.

Then move your attention from the outer body to quieting the soul (mind, will, and emotions), so as to commune with the Holy Spirit. Perhaps you will not need any further steps before you begin to sense God. I have found if we employ the mind in meditating on Scripture, and the imagination through pondering, that the emotions will usually come along for the ride. The conscience may be pricked by a sin consciousness, which will be quelled by the cleansing of confession.

The following are some practices which take us to inward focus.

Calling on the name of Jesus: If we call on the name of Jesus, He will answer and meet with us. You may want to whisper the name of Jesus several times to focus your thoughts. You may pray the simple Jesus prayer which many people through the ages have prayed to focus their attention: "Lord Jesus Christ have mercy upon me." This prayer is softly and slowly spoken (or thought) till the soul senses the sweet presence of Christ.

Picturing Jesus: I often picture Him with me by asking the Holy Spirit where Jesus is with me. When I sense where Jesus is, I then focus my attention on Him thanking and worshiping Him.

Connecting with Holy Spirit: I turn my attention to Holy Spirit by offering praise and thanks to Him for His presence, life and light within me. I focus upon His light within me, giving Him permission to move upon all of my thoughts, senses and emotions. I wait upon Him and then lift up the passage or verse of scripture and begin to ponder in the circular fashion I have described.

The safety of Father: Often Holy Spirit has prompted me to meet with my Heavenly Father in the safety of His arms. My earthly father was a very safe person for me, so it is comforting and helpful as I picture being embraced and loved, to ponder truths about His greatness.

Circular thinking: If you have a pre-selected topic or Scripture for meditation, gently turn your thoughts to it. If not, ask God what He would like to give you today. Record your starting point (scripture, topic, question or thought). Begin to ponder by applying circular thinking (the words repeated slowly over and over in the mind). Pause between each repetition, rest in each repetition, linger, ponder, allowing time for God's interaction within each repetition.

One thought: As you continue on the one thought or line of scripture you will sense a deepening of understanding. This may come in the form of vision, thoughts, emotions taste, touch or smell.

Vision: by way of mental pictures or inward videos.

Thoughts: interjected, spontaneous thoughts. These thoughts are not your thoughts but are much wiser and enlightening.

Flowing emotions: that give a sense of how Father feels.

Taste Touch and Smell: God created all of our senses, and so He may use them to communicate and deepen our understanding as He leads us into all truth through meditation.

Remember, without faith it is impossible to please God, and we must come to God believing that He loves us and desires even more than we do, to communicate and teach us. We are told in the Scripture to Meditate on His word day and night, so our time is well spent, and faith well invested, as we allow Holy Spirit to deepen us in through the process.

Journaling

Record what is coming through words, thoughts, vision, or other senses. As we receive with thankfulness, more will be given. Writing down or recording what is happening, allows us the freedom to keep receiving, knowing we will be able to test and pray over the concepts and thoughts later. Feel free to ask God what He is saying or showing as it is happening. Interact with Him, like you do with a close friend--after all He already knows what you are thinking. As you give voice to your own thoughts you are more able to process the communication flowing between you and God. Your clear questions will be met with His clear response and will give your mind a focal point for deeper meditation.

Conclusion

Worship and give thanks for the time together with God. Honour your heavenly Father for the revelation and time He shared with you. It is always good to go over your previous time of meditation before the next time so that you are in flow as you approach Him for the next conversation.

Through this simple process, I have found deeper understanding of God's eternal biblical truth, which has enriched my personal walk of faith with Jesus. Before I understood the process of meditation, I had a more limited understanding of the scriptures, even though I had read, and memorized them for many years. Through the practice of meditation, my love for God and His written word increased, along with understanding His wisdom and counsel for every-day decisions. The Logos has, in this way, become personal revelation (Rhema). It has quickened my soul, thus becoming part of who I am as well as aligning my life in practical ways to God's truth and will.

God is a wonderful communicator. His desire to commune is greater than ours, and He is very good at removing our barriers. In fact, Holy Spirit once reassured me in a time of self-doubt that God can speak louder than I can listen, so I need not worry that I will be hard of hearing. Our faith is key, but God is in the business of increasing our little faith. After all, faith comes by hearing, and hearing by the word of God. God will increase our faith to receive as we lean on Him to bring us into the depths of friendship. He will reawaken the Garden of Eden within each of us as we take time to be with Him in the cool of the day (the simplicity of quiet moments), just as Adam and Eve once did.

Listening Journaling/Meditation Exercise

Choose a well-known Scripture, for example Psalm 23, and enter into a time of listening prayer or meditation. Spend time on each phrase and go only as far along into the passage as you feel Holy Spirit giving grace to your understanding. You may find that in one hour you will only be able to ponder 5 verses. Don't rush the process. Enjoy the treasures of wisdom and understanding being revealed.

Choose a topic about which you are concerned – take time to meditate and listen to God's perspective.

Choose a relationship for which you need insight, and ask God about His perspective. Write the insights you receive below. NOTE: This is for your understanding only (i.e. not to be used as a letter of correction for the other person(s) involved).

7 – Lectio Divina

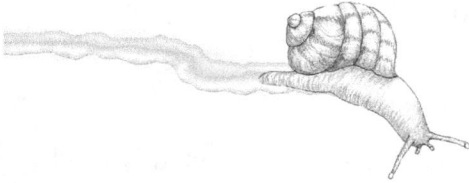

The Latin name Lectio Divina is translated "Reading Divine". This method of meditation was practiced as far back as the 3rd century and was implemented by the Benedictine order. In the 4th century the Desert Fathers began early models of Christian monastic life. These early communities began to practice "constant prayer". The idea behind the practice of Divine Reading is that the Scripture is prayerfully repeated and pondered so that the Holy Spirit may interact with the human spirit to bring enlightenment.

As centuries passed, the practice of Divine Reading became more structured in community (practiced by monks in monasteries). Divine Reading is, however, very suited to individual practice. One description of Lectio Divina is to "feast on the Word." This practice of divine reading is not about how we do the exercise, but more about the goal, which is to connect with God through the Scripture. Reading, meditating, praying and contemplating on the word is not the point. The point of this, as with all spiritual disciplines, is to connect and enjoy Father, Son and Holy Spirit. Fellowship, and even deep intimacy, is our goal, not to have perfection of practice.

Four Steps To Feast On the Word

The first bite of this feast on the word is the "Lecto" step. Then chewing on the word is "Meditatio". Savoring the flavor is "Oratio". Digestion is called "Contemplatio".

Lecto: Read

Find a short passage of Scripture and prayerfully read the passage several times, slowly reciting it and inviting the Holy Spirit to guide you. Read at least 4 times, emphasising different aspects each time. Allow Holy Spirit to guide you in highlighting part, or narrowing down the amount of words you read. You may settle on just a phrase or part of a verse.

Meditatio: Meditate/Reflect

Reflect on the phrase your heart has settled on. Allow it to enter your being to fill your thoughts without judging or analyzing. Perhaps Holy Spirit will give pictures to illuminate your understanding. Feel whatever emotion it elicits in you. Ponder what questions it asks of you. Does the passage inspire, confuse, challenge or convict your heart? Allow the words to read you. Wait for the action of Holy Spirit to do the work of revealing it's meaning for you.

Oratio: Pray/Respond,

Dialogue with God in response to your heart. Talk over the feelings you are experiencing. Ask Him questions and wait for the answers. Express your love and devotion, confess any sin, and come into agreement with His thoughts. Give Him permission to adjust you heart.

Contemplatio: Contemplate/Rest

Ponder in silence, mulling over what God has revealed. St Bernard of Clairvaux compared the process to a kiss by the Eternal Father who allows us to experience union with God. As the Spirit of God kisses each word to our souls, the Living Word changes us. Be still and know He is God. He is near. Here we rest in the presence of God and allow His divine love to wash over and soak us.

Lectio Divina Exercise

Suggested Scripture passages to begin your practice of Lectio Divina: Remember to take only 2 or 3 verses per session.

Psalm1, Psalm 15, Psalm 34, Psalm 42, Psalm 62, Psalm 63, Psalm 84.

Proverbs 24:3 to 5

Matthew 5: 3 to 11 (The Beatitudes)

Matthew 7:7 and 8 (Ask, Seek, Knock)

Mark 14:22 to 25 (Communion)

8 – Journaling

People who heard God's voice in the Bible heard Him through words, pictures, visions, dreams, through nature, and in many other ways. There are prophets in the Bible who were very good at hearing God and one of them tells us exactly how he did it. In Habakkuk 2:1–4 the prophet is describing how he could hear God. At the time, he was upset because he felt God was letting the Babylonians do evil to his people. He wants an answer from God so he tells us what he did.

> *Verse 1: I will stand like a guard and watch. I will wait to see what the Lord will say to me. I will wait and learn how He answers my questions. 2: The Lord answered me, Write it clearly on a sign so that the message will be easy to read. 3: This message is about a special time in the future. This message is about the end and it will come true. Just be patient and wait for it. The time will come; it will not be late. 4: This message cannot help those who refuse to listen to it, but those who are good will live because they believe it. Habakkuk 2:1–4*

First, Habakkuk had to stand still and focus or STOP what he was doing so he could pay attention. Next, He watched or LOOKED to see what God would say...wait a minute... do you look to hear? I think it is more common to look to see but we do hear much better what is actually being said if we look and hear together. We see that Habakkuk LISTENED very carefully. He says in that verse that he will wait and learn the answers to his questions so he is not going to have a quick listen and run off. He is going to take the time to wait and learn. Then in verse 2, God tells him to write the message clearly on tablets so it will be easy to read. God says to be patient and wait for the things He says are going to happen because it will take some time. In verse 4, He tells Habakkuk what to do with the message...let others know and the wise will listen, but some will not and those will be beyond help.

Three Simple Steps to Hearing God's Voice Through Words

As has been said, God wants to speak to us, which He does in many ways. People often need language to solidify and understand concepts, so it is very helpful if we learn to hear God through words. Following are three simple steps to help you hear and then record what God is telling you. First we need to STOP, next we need to LOOK, and then LISTEN. As we listen to God it is best to write down what we hear so we can keep listening and remember everything He says. These three words are a reminder of how to connect with God at any time. Hearing God is simple – childlike in fact. So let's come to Him in childlike faith believing in His desire for us.

Step 1: STOP

Way back in history people realized if they wanted to hear God they needed to slow down, stop talking, and listen up! They gave it the name of 'stillness.' Being still to know God, was practiced by the men and women in the Bible and is mentioned many times. Following are some Bible references which tell us to be quiet, listen to God and meditate on His response: Psalm 2: 1–3, Psalm

27: 14, Psalm 37: 7, Psalm 131: 2, Proverbs 1: 33, Isaiah 40: 29, Hosea 2: 14, Matthew 11: 28–30, Luke 10: 39, Hebrews 4: 9–11.

Becoming still is the process of quieting yourself. We need to quiet the noise around us and within us. We have so many distractions in our lives that we have to make a concentrated effort to stop the noise and be still. Following are some common distractions and how to deal with them.

Allow time: As you learn to relax and meet with God, you will need to dedicate some time to the process. Clock-watching is a distraction that can be removed by setting a timer. Give yourself time to settle into stillness, then some time to listen to God and write down what He is saying. I have found about 30 minutes is a good length of time to begin. As you grow in your times with God it is very easy to spend an hour or more with Him in this focused way. Of course, we need to remember that God is always with us but very often we are not present with Him and attentive to His voice.

Remove outer distractions: Find a place where you will not be disturbed by electronic devices, phones, or the movement of other people or pets. Things you may need are a pen, notepad, a glass of water, and, if you are planning a longer period of time, you may need a pillow and blanket.

Make yourself physically comfortable – find a restful position. If you lay down, choose a position that is different from your normal sleeping position, or guess what will probably happen! For those who feel most relaxed while walking, choose a quiet, solitary place to walk where you can easily relax and focus on God.

Remove inner distractions: Relax. Smile a little. You may want to whisper the name of Jesus several times to focus your thoughts. Perhaps you will not need any further steps before you begin to sense God.

For some, however, this is when the mind begins to flit about or go into activity. Stillness of mind is not emptying the mind of thoughts, but quieting the mind to focus on the presence of Jesus. Don't try to force your mind to be quiet or it probably will try harder to get you thinking. Just listen to the thoughts and see what the issue is. You can ask Holy Spirit, "What are my thoughts?" He will show you. Here is a list of things that cloud our thoughts.

Worry: Give the worry over to God in prayer. Tell Him you trust Him to hold the issue (or person) during your time together. Picture the concern in God's hands and command worry to be silent in the name of Jesus.

The to-do list: Just write the list down, as your mind will feel better knowing you got the message and you will get to the list later.

People to pray for: Even friends in need of prayer must be put on hold for the time being. Just make a note of the names and choose to pray for them later. This is your time to personally connect and hear God's heart for you. Don't let any other need take away from your time with Him.

Sin-consciousness: Guilt can be a barrier to meeting with God. God has provided the ultimate help for us through Jesus. He has more than paid for our sin with His life given on the cross. Just bring your sin to Him and agree with Him for your cleansing and restoration. Receive your forgiveness. Allow Him to wash over you in loving acceptance. As the Bible says, there is no condemnation or separation for God's people. We are welcome to the Father's throne of grace and nothing can separate us from His love.

Remember that condemnation, guilt, and shame are not sent from God. He takes you as you are. By His precious blood, you are now fully accepted into His family as His child and heir. It is now your inheritance to fully enjoy your Father, and for Him to fully enjoy time with you.

The right attitude: Thankfulness and worship (admiration for God and His ways) is the doorway to God's zone. Have faith that God wants to talk to you even more than you want to talk to Him. He is looking forward to sharing thoughts with you and helping you to know Him.

Repent of any negative words: Pray a simple prayer to renounce any negative words that may have hindered you from hearing God. Words such as, "I can't hear God", "God doesn't talk to me" or "Who do you think you are? You can't hear God." Forgive anyone who has said negative words over you. Ask forgiveness for saying and believing that you do not hear God. Receive your forgiveness for any sin that may be disturbing your ability to come to God. Repent for wrong use of your hearing (for example: listening to negative, anti-God, swear words or music). Dedicate your inner ears to God.

Step 2: LOOK

It is so much easier to understand what a person really means if we can see them. Texting is not the best way of communicating, because although it is a fast, almost instant way to talk, you can easily misunderstand the message. Misunderstandings happen when we can't see the expressions and hear the tones of people. There is something important about multi-sensory communication that helps us to hear. The prophets used vision and hearing to get God's message. Jesus only did what He saw his father do[2] and so we can use the eyes of our hearts and our inner ears as we listen to God. The Bible also tells us to fix our eyes on Jesus[3] so using our inner eyes to picture Jesus is biblical and very helpful.

---

2   John 5: 19
3   Hebrews 12:12

Picturing Jesus: You may ask Holy Spirit where Jesus is in the room with you, then focus on His presence. Or you could picture yourself in a comfortable scene with Him, perhaps putting yourself into a Bible scene like being with Jesus at the Sea of Galilee.

Step 3: LISTEN

Ceasing from activity (both outward and inward) and quieting ourselves before God, allows us to listen. Often, when people are learning to hear God, they need to 'oil the wheels' of the inner ears by asking a question.

Some questions you could use are: "How do You see me, God?" or "What do You want to say to me about hearing Your voice, (seeing You, being with You)?" "Jesus speak to me about my friendship with You."

Every morning I begin my day with the question, "What do You want to say to me today, Lord?"

Keep your question simple and open-ended so that you will not be receiving a yes or no answer. God desires to spend time with you and commune with you. Yes or no answers shorten the conversation and are difficult to test. The Lord wants relationship with you and getting to know His heart for you means spending time listening and talking together. You can follow these steps to help you to hear God's voice.

1. **Picture Jesus**: Begin by using the eyes of your heart (your imagination) to picture being with Jesus. Often people find it easier to become childlike seeing themselves as a young child in a well-known scene (for me it is the beach as I grew up as a child spending much time on the beach in Australia).

2. **Ask your question**: Choose any of the questions mentioned previously and wait for flowing

spontaneous thoughts or pictures to come.

3. **Write down the conversation**: It is good to keep a journal of your time with God including dreams, visions, and God's words to you. Date each conversation or God encounter so you can test and re-read them at a later date.

4. **Test what you have heard**: When we are learning a new skill, we usually need a mentor or teacher who is good at the thing we are trying to learn. The advice of more experienced friends will help us grow and stay on track in the new skill of hearing and understanding God's voice. It is a wonderful encouragement and support to have several trusted friends who can help, reassure and show you how to test what you have written or experienced. Ask people who are mature in their faith, already hear God well, that you feel safe sharing with, and who are encouraging and kind.

5. **Confirmation**: You can always ask God to give you confirmation for anything you are unsure of. I have often been given Scripture references (just the book of the Bible and the numbers) which, when I found them in the Bible, confirmed what God had been speaking to me in my time of listening.

Journaling Exercise

Write a letter to God telling Him how you feel about Him, then picture yourself with Jesus and ask Him one of these questions:

How do you see me Jesus? or Talk to me about my friendship with you, God.

Write what you feel, the thoughts that come as well as what you see in the space below your note to God. Use no more than the page below to talk to Him and then use the next page for His answer to you.

9 – Fasting

Because the spiritual discipline of fasting has been practiced for centuries, many differing opinions exist. My personal experience with fasting is certainly not as extensive as some, however, I want to share some insights I have gained.

The title of fasting, given to this practice of denying one's-self in order to draw closer to God is, I feel, almost opposite to what we do in practice to connect with Him. "Slowing" may be a more accurate descriptive name than "fasting". When we stop normal activities and turn our attention toward God, thus slowing down, we remove distractions, hindrances and even normal activities in favour of focusing on Him.

The Purpose of Fasting

Fasting, or abstaining from some daily need, awakens our soul toward God. It draws our attention away from our own needs toward our greater need of Him. The purpose of fasting is not to invoke God's attention or presence; since our Father God does not have a problem with focus or connecting with us, we do not need to fast in order to get His attention! Nor is fasting to be taken on for the purpose of making our case more urgent to Him, or to cause Him to change a circumstance or act on our behalf. If we fast to get something from God, we are actually trying to manipulate Him.

The Benefits of Fasting

Fasting brings focus to life. When we fast, we give undivided attention to God, so that we become keenly aware of His presence. We set aside normal, even very much needed, requirements (e.g. food, drink/, interaction with others). We may also put aside less urgent needs (e.g. our use of the telephone, computer, leisure time, exposure to media, or entertainment). Communion, or time spent in God's presence, brings His divine outlook into focus. We are then able to go back to normal life with better perspective and motivation because we have been aligned to God's plan. Even though our circumstances may not change, we come to them with renewed hope, and many times a fresh strategy.

Fasting can bring death to our flesh, or human, earthly outlook and habits; this, in turn, enables us to live according to the Holy Spirit's direction. This is because our motivation is to allow God to work the submission (or "death") process within us as we yield to His ways (or "life"). We must be careful, however, to keep in mind the potential for defeating the very purpose of fasting: our flawed human nature can lead us down the path of religious pride.

A Word of Caution

Jesus encountered a religious pride in the leaders of His day which seemed to be particularly connected to their practice of regular scheduled fasting. It seems there exists a strong temptation to pride and religious superiority if our choice to fast comes from human decision and not by Holy Spirit's express direction.

I have to confess I have fallen into the same pharisaical spirit when fasting on a schedule. I certainly benefited from the bodily discipline of abstaining from food when appropriate, and I did draw near to God during those times. However, I was also convicted by Holy Spirit of pride and religiosity. Though it has been thought of as a wonderful discipline to deny one's self, self-abasement can actually become self-focused as we turn toward ourselves and our accomplishments instead of toward the person of Jesus Christ.

Contemporary Fasting

A food/ drink fast, though it is severe and difficult, may not be as effective in today's Western world as fasting from what captures our focus and attention. Abstaining from media, telecommunications, computer use and interaction with other people, may in fact be much more effective in our goal of turning our full attention toward God. I suspect that, for many people, such a fast would be more of a challenge than going without meals.

Let us, for example, imagine that we stop eating and drinking, but continue to answer the phone, send text messages, read email, tweet our thoughts, or catch up on Facebook. Our food fast would certainly not bring the desired benefits, because we have not stilled and quieted our souls. The latter is what counts!

Though I have enjoyed seasons of regular food fasting, I have more recently found that slowing down to spend days apart for personal retreat is what proves to be the most effective way to "fast".

Indeed, for many, the most important spiritual practices are the disciplines of solitude and silence. Through solitude we learn the practice of intentionally being alone. Through silence we learn the practice of being quiet. Solitude and silence are critical in our hyper-connected world. With the constant barrage of information and communication, it's virtually impossible to turn off the noise and busyness without being intentional.

In such a spirit of dedication, we need to commit to put aside all technology, media, and social activity to be alone with God. When it comes to seeking Him, that choice is most fruitful.

I do fast from food when Holy Spirit directs me. From my experience, this kind of fasting is more often for consecration to a new work, or at the beginning of a new season in my life. Whether food is part of the fast is not as important as my motivation and dedication to being with God, away from outside influences and distractions.

Meditation/Journaling Exercise
Please speak to me about fasting. What kind of fasting would enhance my connection with You Jesus?

Purpose to set aside a period of time to connect with God through the fasting He has recommended for your growth.

10 – Retreat

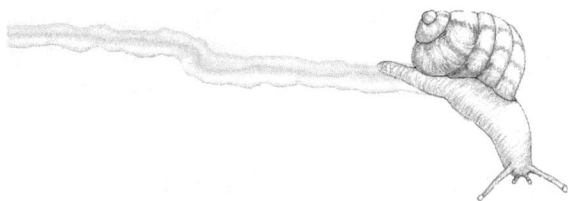

To come away with God, spending some time in quietness and solitude is, in a sense, a fast from the "normal" life. Welcome these times of slowing down, as God's invitation to draw near and give undivided focus to Him. Retreating into the presence of God can be done anywhere – even right in your own home, however, I have found when we intend to take time away from home, work, and family it is best to be in a different location. If we go to a peaceful place, where we are not constantly fighting the temptation to step back into everyday thoughts, time awareness, and habits, focus on God is much easier.

I find a personal retreat becomes a like a pilgrimage of sorts. Once I have begun traveling to the place where I will spend my retreat, God begins to show me things. From the moment I step out of my door till I step back in upon return, God is sharing His heart and often unveiling mine. It seems that God waits excitedly for us to come away and draw near to Him. He orchestrates wonderful encounters with all kinds of signs and spiritual metaphors encrypted into messages.

I record in my journal everything that captures my attention on my journey, and at the place of retreat, so none will be lost. It is such a pleasure to ponder each treasure and to marvel at the manifold ways He communicates. Retreat allows time to get lost in thinking of Jesus. When we are away from familiar things, with no work or agenda to fill time, we allow ourselves to take the tangents Holy Spirit suggests. I love to walk, noting God's voice through nature. All creation sings His song. Having times of silence allows for drinking-in His whisperings and noticing each natural sound around me. Everything echoes the Voice and the Presence. Even meals can become symbolic representations God will use. The flavours and fragrance of God resound if I take time to notice.

So, I encourage you to take the times of retreat as Holy days with God to deepen the awareness, understanding and intimacy of your friendship with God.

Meditation/Journaling Exercise
How would You, Lord, like to spend extended times with me?

Purpose to plan a retreat with God. Actively arrange the details according to God's recommendations.

11 – Pilgrimage

A pilgrimage to any destination can become a spiritual marker, which can change the course of our lives. It's not often we hear spiritual pilgrimage talked about today. Perhaps because travel is not the arduous adventure it once was. We take long trips in our stride. In previous centuries, people embarked on marathon pilgrimages to exotic places, at great peril to their lives. For many it was life or death to them to make the journey to places like the Holy Land. Many devoted people still do take costly trips, lengthy trips in hopes of touching the divine. Books have been written of actual pilgrimages as well as allegorical tales, such as Pilgrims Progress, written by Paul Bunion. It seems the spiritual significance of the journey is the mysterious link between events, people, places and the puzzle God strings together in the process of an actual real-time journey.

We see in Scripture many examples of journeys, which have natural significance for the travelers. Many of these journeys also have spiritual significance – not just to the people who took them, but even to those who read about it centuries later. Most of the characters from Scripture were unaware they were on pilgrimage, but often their journeys became one. As we attune to God's intention in their travels, we may find, like them, the voice and presence of God pointing the way into places more significant than we have imagined.

A Significant Journey from Genesis: Noah

The opening words of the account of Noah tell us volumes: Noah was a righteous man, blameless among the people. The people he lived among were wicked, violent and grieved the heart of God. Somehow Noah managed to be different. If we back up a verse we see how: But Noah found favour in the eyes of the Lord. Favour is not only about the blessings of health, wealth, power and such, it is much more importantly about keeping us in alignment with God's ways and nature. Even though corruption and evil polluted the world around him Noah was drawn to God. He walked with God. God shared His grief over what people became and Noah seemed to understand. Noah didn't argue or try to convince God to spare the earth. We are told he did everything just as God commanded him, every detail.

What a process that obedience took him on! Just the building of the ark probably took 100 years, then came the catastrophic flood which the earth had never (will never again) see the likes of. The time in the ark was 370 days, which were surely difficult to endure because of the many unknowns. The story of this humble, simple man, who was a friend of God, did all that the Lord commanded, shows strength and courage. I can imagine the opposition was strong; with arguments against Noah building a huge boat, miles from any body of water. Then the warnings urging people to escape the worldwide flood must have caused much mockery, since people hadn't ever seen rain.

Many signs were given; one of which was the miracle of the creatures coming to Noah. I'm sure it was a sight to behold; all the animals streaming into the ark. You would think that would cause more than a second look from the bystanders, but no one got it. It seems human nature hasn't changed. Think about that. If the same sign was given today how many would get it. Doesn't Jesus say something about that?

"As it was in the days of Noah so it will be at the coming of the Son of Man." Matthew 24:37

Signs are given but we miss them, unless we are tuned in to the director of our Journey.

Further Signs

The Wind: We are told during the long days of waiting and drifting, the wind God sent caused the waters to recede. Wind symbolizes the Spirit of God (as in the beginning, before God created Man His Spirit hovered over the waters. God was bringing a new beginning through the wind that once again brought forth the dry land as He did in the beginning.

The Birds: Noah released birds, testing the readiness of the land, reminiscent of the 5th day of creation when birds were created and released by the Spirit of God over the newly created land. The number five is the number of grace. Grace was given to Noah and family to have a second chance – a new beginning.

The Raven: 40 days after the rain stopped, Noah released a raven. The black raven represents the unclean or sinful man, finding no place to rest. Forty represents a time of testing.

The Dove was released after the raven, but it could not find a resting place. Noah waited 7 days then sent the same dove. This time it came back to him with a freshly plucked olive leaf. He waited another week and released the dove again. This time it didn't return as it had found a place to nest. The symbolism of the dove represents Holy Spirit released. First there was no place for Him in the earth because of sin. After 7 days (God's time for re-creation fulfilled) the olive branch comes to Noah, which represents the reconciliation made by Christ through his sacrifice for sin.

The final seven days is the time of Holy Spirit living in His home on earth. We who carry Holy Spirit are the resting place where Holy Spirit finds His rest.

Noah was in tune. The favour he had (which is also God's mercy) gave grace so that he could walk with God. We can be favoured to walk with God too. He is longing to encompass us with His protective, productive love. Noah sure was productive! Noah built a huge boat – but even more significantly, he was the foundation of a new society. Are we called to any less? Perhaps our part is just a drop in the bucket of God's kingdom on earth. Nevertheless, it is uniquely our part, and we get to build it, like Noah, just as God commanded him, from a humble heart of obedient love.

You can see the significance of this pilgrimage through the interpretation of the symbols that appeared during the journey. So it is with every spiritual journey we embark on. If we will pay attention, God will speak. Attentiveness to the natural happenings and inward stirring of Holy Spirit bring revelation of what God is saying. Keeping a written journal is essential when on a pilgrimage, so we can capture every hint He gives. Often it is not till I've returned home that the full interpretation is revealed to me. The beauty of pilgrimage is the enjoyment of the journey and later unwrapping the sweet mystery which has unfolded along the way.[4]

Meditation/Journaling Exercise
What do You say Jesus about us taking a spiritual pilgrimage?

Take the opportunity to journey with God. Remember it is not the destination that matters but being with Him as you travel.

---

4 For Other Journeys in Genesis: Abraham (Gen: 12 to 22), Lot (Gen: 13 to 14), Jacob (Gen: 27 to 35), Joseph (Gen: 37 to 45)

12 – Sacred Hours

In monastic communities, across denominations, with differing emphasis we see times of day and night being used as reminders to pray. The watches of the night are spoken of in the Old Testament.

> *On my bed I remember you; I think of you through the watches of the night. Psalm 63:6*

> *My eyes stay open through the watches of the night, that I may meditate on your promises. Psalm 119:148*

> *Arise, cry out in the night, as the watches of the night begin: pour out your heart like water in the presence of the Lord. Lift up your hands to him for the lives of your children, who faint from hunger at every street corner. Lamentations 2:19*

When Jesus was approaching His greatest time of trial on earth, He encouraged His disciples to watch and pray that they would be able to escape all that is about to happen and that they would be able to stand against temptation (Luke 12:36). This encouragement from Him fell on drowsy ears in the garden of Gethsemane, whilst Jesus agonized in prayer alone.

With these and other examples from Scripture in mind, men and women of devotion have used appointed times as calls to prayer. Some communities have developed beautiful traditions of appointed hours of prayer for specific purposes. Times of prayer vary in when they occur, as well as the number of times per 24-hour period. The hours have traditional names but again these can vary. Listed next is an example of the Divine Hours with times, their names and some of the prayer focus people have practiced.

- **6:00pm Vespers**: Marks the end of the day's work. All our burdens of the day are brought to God. We ask forgiveness and healing for what we have done and what we have failed to do.

- **9:00pm Compline**: This hour is a time of 'closing day' prayer. The darkness is a friend, as the presence of God comforts us through the night.

- **12:00am Midnight, sometimes called Matins**: The midnight hour prayer time was for protection and thanksgiving for the laws of God. Psalm 119:62–64 At midnight I rise to give you thanks for your righteous law.

- **3:00 am Vigils**: Rising to pray at Vigils is difficult, but fruitful. The term prayer vigil is often used to speak of all-night prayer. Praying at Vigils is often focused on prayer for family protection and increased personal devotion.

- **6:00 am Lauds**: Marks the coming of the new day. Often thought to be the time of resurrection. Rising from the dark of night into newness of life.

- **9:00am Terce**: The workday begins and thanks are given for the ability to labour. Unity is celebrated as the community joins to accomplish a common goal. During this hour, prayer, thanksgiving and dedication of health, strength, work, and co-labourers was often offered.

- **12:00 noon Sext**: Midday prayer was a time of thanksgiving, rest and reflection. Time for checking of hearts alignment to the Son of Righteousness. After the meal there is a time of silence and reflection before work is resumed.

- **3pm None:** Time at lengthening shadows mid to late afternoon. The reality that things don't last forever – time moves on. We let go of the things that have caused darkness and shadows in our lives and pay attention to eternal enduring things. Prayer of releasing the old and embracing the new.

These sacred hours have helped people to stop the treadmill of living, to remember the Divine presence with them. They can be a reminder to us, if we choose to practice them that God is here with us in every moment. These interruptions of prayer help us to remember He is interested and involved in our work, leisure, and even our sleep. God is still, and always will be, present in our space and time, willing to listen to our prayers. Perhaps He has been initiating this discipline with you. In my journey with Jesus I did have a season of waking at the watches of the night. I was quite intrigued to find that this spiritual practice was well used in convents and monasteries for centuries. God takes us through these intimate times of call to prayer, to grow our spirits and develop us into His mature sons, a bride fit for her king. He is ready to love, comfort and encourage us with His still small voice, as we devote time and attention to Him. May we rise with Him in the watches of the night and join our beloved in prayer.

Meditation/Journaling Exercise
How might practicing specific times of prayer enhance my practice of your presence?

What might those times be God, and how would you want me to spend them?

13 – Walking

When walking with a friend we probably would not enjoy a one-way talk, our friend doing all the talking, with them asking questions with no expectation that we would give an answer. Imagine listening to their list of many requests for our help with no thought of stopping to hear our response. It would be a rare person who would want to accompany that friend. Probably only a counsellor would consider another walk with them, but even at that, if the friend is not listening to the advice, the counsellor would also have a frustrating walk. Think about how most of us view prayer walking. Is it not that we do all the talking, asking God to help us and others, even begging that He intervene? That method of prayer walking is usually not very relaxing or enlightening, but is probably what most of us do because we have not thought of walking in prayer as relaxing.

When I first began prayer walking, I did not realize Holy Spirit led prayers are most the effective. I assumed I should pray for the area I was walking in, making petitions on behalf of the people living there. I focused on telling God things He knew, and asking Him to fix this and that. I didn't relax and get a feel for what He might want to talk about. My focus was on doing the work of prayer rather that enjoying the One who is the answer. I have learned (and am still learning) to let go of doing the praying, in favour of sensing, listening and looking for what God is saying. My inward stance was using my knowledge, and sometimes my physical senses, to figure out how to pray for people in the area where I was walking. I used the time to express my thoughts to God, instead of allowing the Holy Spirit to express His thoughts in me. There are still times I go out for a walk to pray for people, but now I allow Him to align my heart, so I pray as He wants me to. Then as I ask, in the name of Jesus, He will answer my request because it is according to His will. (John 14: 14)

Prayer Walking to Connect With Jesus

Walking in an attitude of prayer is a better way to think of positioning ourselves to relate to God as we go out. Walking with God will come to be a beautiful way to relax and listen to Him. With an adjusted attitude we can allow ourselves to turn our minds to pondering, especially if we can enjoy a beautiful natural setting where we are surrounded by sights and sounds of nature. The outdoors, fresh air and the steady rhythmic pace of the walking is a wonderful de-stressor for most of us, so it is meant to be that we can enjoy the presence of Christ with us, as we inwardly still ourselves and walk in His presence.

A contemplative or meditative walk is quite different from practicing these disciplines in our usual indoor place. If we are outside, we will need to pay attention to the voice of God speaking through the surroundings as well as internally speaking through spontaneous thoughts or visions. Pondering a scripture or question will be more effective as we take note of things highlighted through our natural senses (sight, hearing, touch, taste, and smell). We may also have emotional experiences that are not usual for us at that moment such as joy, sadness, fear, anger, or compassion. These emotions could be God's way of highlighting what is behind our ponderings and prayers. In all of these differing experiences God can be unfolding fresh understanding. Interacting with God as we walk is often like a mini pilgrimage. It is important to write down what we have noted and experienced on our walk, so as to relish all the walk with Him has given.

The Labyrinth

Of course, we don't need structure to the walk to tap into the presence of God, but it can be fun and enlightening to experience the practice of walking the Labyrinth. Though the Labyrinth is not a maze in the pure sense of the word, it does resemble some of its characteristics. There are no tricks and no dead end, as would be in a maze, but it does have geometric form. The labyrinth has a single path that winds its way into the center. The person walking the Labyrinth uses the same path to return from the center and exits through the place where they began. There is only one pathway one can take, there are no walls hiding the correct pathway from view as would be in a maze, but the idea of walking the Labyrinth did originate from the ancient maze.

Labyrinth designs have been found on pottery, tiles and walls at least 5,000 years ago. Patterns are based on spirals, circles and natural shapes. The Celts said the labyrinth was the "Never Ending Circle". In medieval times, they appeared on church walls and floors. They are thought to be an alternative for the common people to taking pilgrimage to the Holy Land. There are early depictions of pilgrims following the maze on their knees while praying.

Labyrinths are currently used as a way to quiet the mind, recover balance in life, encourage insight through listening prayer, and just to simply connect with Gods presence in the current moment.

A Guide to Walking the Labyrinth:

There are some rules to this walk which will enhance your time. You must begin and end the walk at the entrance. Respect others as they walk by not brushing past them, and remain silent. You may stop at any point but be mindful that others may need to pass, so allow room for them. To prepare, you may want to sit quietly and reflect. Ask yourself what you are desiring from your time with God today.

Three stages of the walk:

1. Releasing on the way in: Position our hearts to dedicate the time to God. Let go of preconceived ideas and burdens. Give each worry and negative thought to Him. Become attentive to the present moment.

2. Receiving in the centre: Rest in the moment. Tune into listening with all of our senses. Notice the breeze, your surroundings, the sounds, smells, and emotions and begin to reflect on His presence. Take in and receive God's thoughts and His love.

3. Returning back: Carry back into the world what you have received. Ponder the ways He is affecting your perspective and how it will integrate into your thoughts and life. How will you be different? What new concepts have shifted your thinking?

Even children can enjoy the labyrinth. With some help, they will also receive from the meditative aspects of the walk. The labyrinth is a path of prayer for all people, an opportunity to walk in the presence of Jesus Christ. It can be a place of refreshment and encounter with life changing results as well as just a beautiful way to celebrate the presence of God in each step.

Meditation/Journaling Exercise
Lord please speak to me about walking in attentiveness to Your presence.

Take a walk with God. Be conscience of His voice through the things around you. Remember to record and interpret what you notice.

14 – Singing

Singing is a spiritual practice recommended in Scripture and practiced down through the ages. As we examine singing as a vehicle to encounter the presence of God, we need to remember that singing hymns and spiritual songs was used for many reasons.

Song Creates Atmosphere

Here we note; God uses the songs of stars and angels as a backdrop for Creation.

> *"Where were you when I laid the earth's foundation? Tell me, if you understand. Who marked off its dimensions? Surely you know! Who stretched a measuring line across it? On what were its footings set, or who laid its cornerstone—while the morning stars sang together and all the angels shouted for joy? Job 38:4–7*

Song Can Bring Deliverance

Deliverance for our souls, from interference, can be enacted as the word of God comes to us through songs composed and spontaneously sung as a prophetic declaration over an individual or group. Songs of deliverance were freedom-bringing songs for Israel, and also for those who are oppressed today. There were also battle and victory songs.

> *"People cry out under a load of oppression; they plead for relief from the arm of the powerful. But no one says, 'Where is God my Maker, who gives songs in the night, Job 35:9–10*

> *Therefore, let all the faithful pray to you while you may be found; surely the rising of the mighty waters will not reach them. You are my hiding place; you will protect me from trouble and surround me with songs of deliverance. Psalm 32:6–7*

> *After consulting the people, Jehoshaphat appointed men to sing to the Lord and to praise him for the splendour of his holiness as they went out at the head of the army, saying:*

> *"Give thanks to the Lord, for his love endures forever."*

> *As they began to sing and praise, the Lord set ambushes against the men of Ammon and Moab and Mount Seir who were invading Judah, and they were defeated. 2 Chronicles 20:21–22*

Song Creates an Atmosphere to Receive From God

In this text we see the barren woman is to sing before she is healed so she activates faith to receive the children she longs for.

> *"Sing, barren woman, you who never bore a child; Burst into song, shout for joy, you who*

were never in labour; because more are the
children of the desolate woman than of her
who has a husband," says the Lord. Isaiah
54:1

Song Teaches, Instructs and Admonishes

There is a richness which envelopes the teaching and admonition of the word when we sing it.

> *Let the message of Christ dwell among*
> *you richly as you teach and admonish one*
> *another with all wisdom through psalms,*
> *hymns, and songs from the Spirit, singing*
> *to God with gratitude in your hearts. And*
> *whatever you do, whether in word or deed,*
> *do it all in the name of the Lord Jesus, giving*
> *thanks to God the Father through him.*
> *Colossians 3:16–17*

Singing in congregational/group settings has been a vehicle for voicing the gospel of redemption, teaching doctrine, making commitments to creeds and biblical truth, as well as for praise and worship of God. Singing scripture gives not only the repetition people require to memorize, but it allows us the opportunity to ponder the deeper meaning of the words and gives Holy Spirit time to do the surgery those words are meant to do. Often tears flow as conviction and tenderness wells up in us because of Holy Spirit's anointing of a song.

There is indeed spiritual power in music that is foundational to our growth in God. As we vocalize gratitude, thanksgiving, and honour to God we speak the truth of who God is, reminding ourselves of His kindness and power. As we sing, we remind ourselves that God is here with us that we belong to Him and He is keeping us by His power. We tell ourselves the truth. Even if we don't feel it is true, the melody and repetition goes to a deep, heart level and works to re-ignite truth to us.

We sing the songs passed down to us through scriptures and tradition. As we learn new truths and affirm those we hold dear, the texts and music become part of us, giving us the language of faith, of prayer and of witness, connecting with us on emotional and spiritual levels.

Singing as a meditative practice has been part of traditional communities for centuries. The beauty of Gregorian Chants echo's down to us and can be used by the Holy Spirit to inspire love and devotion in this present generation. The repetition of modern worship songs is reminiscent of the chant and is quite meditative also. The repetition allows us to forget about the mechanics of getting notes and words correct, freeing us to enter into the meaning of the song, bringing depth of insight and passion for God.

Singing in one's prayer language is very meaningful to the soul and spirit, though the mind may not comprehend. Ecstatic singing brings great delight in expressing the love for God that our words cannot articulate. The song of the heart is a song deeper than human words – it is a heart to heart communication through Holy Spirit to God. It is a wonderful experience to be lost in love and song to Jesus Christ, and is truly a gift to our souls not to mention a delight to our God.

The words of the following hymn were penned by a man who had longed to serve the Lord in ministry, yet was denied for many years due to a mistake about his identity. George Croly was forced to pursue a secular career that was productive in stretching his abilities as a writer and speaker. He wrote this hymn after he had at last become an Anglican minister. It seems to me a song from deep within his loving heart of dedication and humble thanks to God for all he was called to go through.

Holiness Desired

Spirit of God, descend upon my heart; Wean it from earth thro' all its pulses move; Stoop to my weakness, mighty as Thou art, and make me love thee as I ought to love.

I ask no dream, no prophet ecstasies, no sudden rending of the veil of clay, no angel visitant, on opening skies; but take the dimness of my soul away.

Hast Thou not bid us love Thee, God and King? All, all thine own soul, heart, and strength and mind! I see Thy cross there teach my heart to cling; O let me seek Thee, and O let me find!

Teach me to feel that Thou art always nigh; Teach me the struggles of the soul to bear, To check the rising doubt, the rebel sigh; Teach me the patience of unanswered prayer.

Teach me to love Thee as Thine angles love, One holy passion filling all my frame; The baptism of the heav'n descended Dove – My heart an altar, and Thy love the flame.

George Croly 1854

This Hymn is such a reminder to us of what is really central to communion with God. It is not the ecstatic experiences of dreams, visions and angelic visitations that need to captivate us. It is just pure love and devotion to know God and live in complete agreement with him. Being authentic and devoted to living at one with God is the goal and focus where every heart will find abiding rest and satisfaction in daily life.

Exercise in Song

In a time of solitude practice singing to God in worship. Experiment with tunes and words that bubbling up from your heart of love for Him. You may sense Him singing over you, express His prophetic song to you through your voice.

Ask God to speak to and through your voice in psalms, hymns and spiritual songs, then open you heart and mouth in expressions of adoration.

15 – Present Jesus

As we began this book, so we shall close, by turning our attention to practicing the presence of God. Jesus is our example, our teacher, our healer, and our present mentor. By His Spirit He indwells us, giving us the closest of all relationships. Jesus is, as we have said throughout this writing, the Life, the Truth and the Way and as such, He is the answer to our spiritual needs, longings and aspirations.

I have found the practice of picturing Jesus with me in the present moment, to be the most helpful of all practices in centring my soul. Especially when I am troubled or lack peace. This practice allows me to present the emotions and unrest to God, which frees me from them. There is spiritual power and real substance in the *realized* presence of Christ – in our now moment. When I practice His presence (by picturing) I find release from the issues I present to Him. I have also noticed greater confidence in my experience of His voice. Though Jesus is always present, for He is omnipresent, I am not always aware of that fact. Picturing Him is actually seeing the truth of His presence with me, especially as we allow Holy Spirit to guide us into the practice.

Often my soul struggles to connect with the presence of God due to my feelings of unworthiness or emotional unrest. Of course, none of us is worthy or perfect at any time so, acting on these feelings will keep us from enjoying the truth, of His presence with us always. As we present to Jesus our shortcomings, faults and unrest, He takes each issue and forgives, heals, and releases us from them.

Giving Jesus Negativity

In order to give up negative emotions, thoughts, or distractions we can simply picture Jesus with us. I ask Holy Spirit to help me by asking:

"Holy Spirit please show me where Jesus is with me right now?

When I get a sense of the location the Spirit has given, I focus my imagination on seeing Him there. Holy Spirit is active in this process enabling me to "see Jesus". Once I have the "still picture" Holy Spirit will many times bring the picture to life, then I often see details I have not imagined. These details have, over the years, taught me what God would like to share with me. For example; Jesus clothing will tell me the subject He would like to discuss (gardening hat would be about my spiritual garden).

In the times I need to let go of negativity or emotional unrest, I will sense the problem I want to give to Jesus as some kind of object. For example: I have seen problems as a backpack, a heavy over coat, a bag of garbage, a basket of rotten fruit and such, all of which I give to Him or I may have asked Him to take. As you do this exercise, take time to see the transaction take place, watch what Jesus does with it. Let God talk about how you feel, if needed. I had the experience once of being concerned that worms of bitterness I had given to Jesus, would come out of the hole He had put them in. When I expressed that concern to Jesus, He poured some gasoline into the hole and set it alight, which put my concerns to rest. I experienced a complete release from the bitterness I had been carrying. We are able to experience a truly supernatural healing of emotional turmoil by presenting our issues to Jesus. He is

Truth, so an encounter with truth sets us free.

Ask Jesus What He Will Give to Replace Negativity

Once the problem is given over, we no longer own it, we can if we choose to, ask Jesus what He wants to replace it with. Once again, allow time to receive what is given, as well as time to interpret the gift. Remember to write out what God has done. Sometimes people will be given a positive character trait or emotion such as joy, victory or honesty. At other times we will be given a symbolic gift, which we may need to ponder in depth. The practice of picturing Jesus and presenting Him our cares is a fulfillment of Scripture:

> *Cast all your anxiety on him because he cares for you. 1 Peter 5:7*

> *Cast your cares on the LORD and he will sustain you; he will never let the righteous be shaken. Psalm 55:22*

Let us fix our eyes, focusing our attention, beholding Jesus, who is the author and perfector of our faith. These thoughts have inspired this poem Holy Spirit and I penned together.

Being Present
Moment by moment,
Days spent apart,
Hearing my Saviour speak, straight to my heart.
My deepest longing,
My greatest desire,
To notice God always, and kindle loves fire.
The frail human soul
It wonders distracted,

Will find her attention, fulfilled, love enraptured

Thank You

It is my prayer that you have found this book helpful in your friendship with God. I would love to hear from you and it would be most helpful to have feedback. I encourage you to write a review to help other readers decide on this book.

Other Books

The Language of Dreams and Visions
A Handbook for Interpretation and Symbolism.

This handbook is a guide to understanding and interpreting dreams and visions. It contains an extensive and valuable dictionary of biblical and cultural symbols giving insight into God's way of communication. It includes a template dream journal for recording and interpreting dreams.

Chapters include:

- God Is Speaking
- Supernatural Encounters
- Defining Dream and Vision
- Restoring Dream and Visionary Capacities
- Soaking or Listening Prayer
- Dream and Vision Recording
- Interpretation
- Testing Revelation
- Dictionary of Symbols
- Biblical Reference Section for Dreams, Visions and Bible References for the Names of God

Listen Up!
Discerning the voice of God for your everyday life.

Jesus said, "My sheep know My voice" – and you can tune in and hear from God every day. You will find in this little book practical and easy-to-understand keys for unlocking the door to knowing God's voice. As you read and work through the listening prayer exercises, you will find the pleasure of knowing the One who made you. God has a beautiful plan for your life and you can discover His voice, take His lead, and follow the path Jesus has marked out for you.

Chapters include:

- Hearing With More Than Ears: The Ways God Speaks
- The Faith Factor: The Key That Unlocks Supernatural Life

Stop Look & Listen: Journaling Your Conversations With God

- Discerning Direction: Knowing What the Signs Say
- Christian Meditation: Using The Grey Matter and More
- Checking It Out: God? Satan? Or Just Wishful Thinking?
- How Others Have Learned to Listen Up

The Restoration Manual

A Guide to Restoring the Soul Through Inner-Healing

Developed from Biblical techniques, this approach to prayer counselling is used for Inner Healing of the personality or soul. It is a practical tool to enable every Christian to pray through areas of blockage and emotional pain. Once learned, this method can be used in subsequent areas of emotional pain and blockages to continue on the road of healing and restoration using a free workbook download.

Chapter Headings:

- The Wounded Soul
- Seven Steps for Restoring the Soul
- Restoring Generational Lines
- Correcting Soul Ties
- Healing Painful Memories
- Renouncing Negative Words

- Renewing Truth and Purpose
- Cleansing from the Demonic
- Living by Holy Spirit's Power
- Aftercare
- Leaders Tools

The Kingdom Within

Knowing God the Spirit and learning to flow in and through Him.

This book is for people looking for a primer on Holy Spirit (Holy Spirit 101). It will help you to learn about His nature, graces and gifts but even more importantly it is designed to draw you into a deeper friendship with God. It provides practical and easy ways for you to tune your heart to Him. Each chapter has suggested meditation questions which are designed to enable you to understand what God has for you.

Chapters include:

- Coming to Know the Holy Spirit ~ Progressing Toward Union With God
- Knowing Holy Spirit ~ His Name, Symbolic Descriptions, The Sevenfold Spirit
- Holy Spirit the Giver ~ Fruit of the Spirit, Gifts of the Spirit
- Positioned to Receive ~ Focus, Faith, Filled With the Spirit
- Revealer of Truth ~ How God Speaks, Our Spiritual Senses
- Spiritual Disciplines ~ Listening Prayer, Meditation, Fasting, Spiritual Retreat
- Testing Revelation
- Ministering through the Spirit ~ Praying Like Jesus, Releasing the Flow
- Teamwork ~ Prophetic Etiquette, Seeking God Together

Destiny Purpose and Calling

Understanding and Fulfilling Your Unique Place in God's Kingdom on Earth

A straight-forward, practical guide to bring you along in your journey of discovery as to who God has designed you to be, where you are in your journey of purpose in Him and what you next step along His path is. Every chapter includes action steps to intentionally move you into your purpose and calling so you may enjoy the journey into Kingdom destiny.

Chapters include:

- The Books of Destiny – My Legacy
- Created for Purpose
- Kingdom Calling
- Check the Baggage
- Personal Identity – Where Have I Come From? Who am I? Why am I Here?
- Gifts From God – Discerning My Spiritual Gifts
- Talents & Skills – Discerning My Abilities
- Additions or Distractions
- Tracking With God – Where am I @?
- Finding My Life in Him – Where am I Going?
- Getting to My Destination

About Yvonne

Once a native of Australia, Yvonne lives and works in Canada. She has been married to her husband Bob for more than 45 years. They have five grown children and eight adorable grandchildren. Yvonne has been a friend of God for over 40 years and is growing to love Him more each year. Under God's direction and anointing Yvonne produces:

Rev. Yvonne Prentice,

Pastor at His Presence Ministries

Credentialed with ECCiC

- Customized prayer blankets
- Scripture meditation CD's
- Manuals & books on topics such as inner-healing, listening prayer, meditation, interpreting dreams and visions, knowing the Holy Spirit, and discerning destiny

Yvonne brings encouragement and hope to many. She loves to introduce others to the practice of "soaking" or listening prayer, and Biblical meditation. She loves to foster times in God's presence helping others deepen their friendship with Jesus Christ. Regularly ministering at retreats and workshops, Yvonne's heart is to see God's people grow in intimacy with Jesus Christ by practicing His presence daily.

Contact

Email: hispresenceministries@gmail.com

Facebook: through her page His Presence Ministries.

Blog: pushingtheedges.blogspot.com